SPALDING®

COACHING HOCKEY

Dr. Gerald A. Walford
&
Gerald E. Walford

MASTERS PRESS
SPORTS PUBLISHER

A Division of Howard W. Sams & Co.

Published by Masters Press
(A Division of Howard W. Sams & Co.)
2647 Waterfront Parkway E. Dr., Suite 300
Indianapolis, IN 46214

Printed in the United States of America

Library of Congress Cataloging-in-Publication Data

Walford, Gerald A.
Coaching Hockey / Gerald A. Walford and Gerald E. Walford
      p.   cm. — (Spalding sports library)
      ISBN: 0-940279-79-7
      1. Hockey — Coaching. I. Walford, Gerald E.
      II. Title. III. Series
GV848.25.W33   1993   93-43065
796.962'07'7 -- dc 20   CIP

CREDITS:
Cover design by Lynne Annette Clark
Cover photo by Frank S. Howard
Diagrams by Lisa Barnett and Julie Biddle
Type design by Leah Marckel
Edited by H. W. Kondras

Contents

Section 1

Hockey Fundamentals

Fundamentals are the basis of any game or sport. The fundamentals of hockey are skating, puck control and goaltending.

Team strategy and game control depends on the effectiveness of fundamentals. Passing plays are of little value if the passing and pass receiving are weak. In fact, if a team cannot pass or receive a pass, the team cannot control the game. Skating, passing and pass receiving are vital to the team. This section is the basis for the team strategy section.

1. Skating
2. Puck Control
3. Goaltending

1

SKATING

Skating is the foundation of hockey. Good and poor hockey players are separated more by skating ability than any other factor. Good skaters are able to execute and learn passing, shooting, and stickhandling skills more easily than poor skaters.

There are two main styles of skating — forward and backward. Each style is divided into free style and agility skating.

SKATING AND RUNNING— A COMPARISON

When learning to skate, beginners move to a walking or running stride. Although this may be a natural reaction, it is far from correct. Skating and running are entirely different. In running, the leg and foot move forward, and touch the ground under the body's center of gravity. The leg then pushes back, straight back and in line with the direction of travel.

In skating, the leg moves under the body and glides forward with the toe pointing in the direction of travel. The knee then leads the leg and foot in rotating outward as the leg pushes to the side of the direction of travel. At the maximum extension of the leg, the push is completed and the leg swings around and back under the body for the glide.

In running there is no outward rotation of the leg as there is in skating. If one was to stand behind a runner and observe the running action, it would be readily noticeable that the legs move straight forward and backward. Stand behind a skater and watch him skate away and one will notice that the legs rotate in a circular motion. The following illustration shows the circular action.

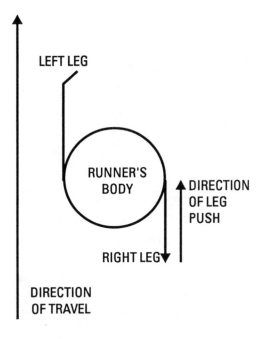

Figure 1-1:Running Action

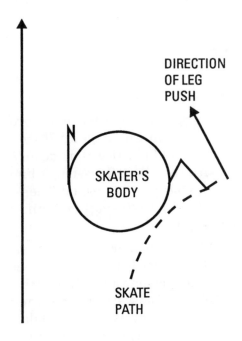

Figure 1-2:Skating Action

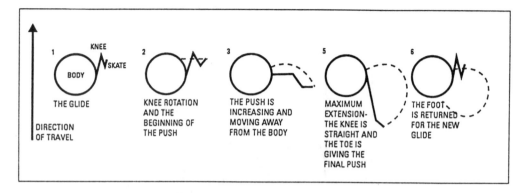

Figure 1-3: Circular Leg Action

Another important difference between skating and running is the upper body action. A runner's shoulder action is diagonal to his leg action, while the skater utilizes similar shoulder and leg action. When the runner's right leg is forward the left shoulder and left arm swing forward. When skating, the right shoulder and right arm swing forward with the forward right leg action.

When running, a person's feet are both off the ground at the same time. In skating, one foot is always in contact with the ice. The runner runs on a friction surface as the foot does not slip or slide on the running surface. The skater skates on a frictionless surface for a sliding and slippery action with the skate blade.

FORWARD SKATING

The Upper Body

The head maintains an upright position. It does not drop, droop, bob or tilt. It also maintains a constant distance from the ice. If one were to watch a good skater from the side, one would notice that despite the bending and straightening of the legs, the head will flow along a line level to the ice and remain at that level as long as the speed is constant. The skater's head and neck do not shift from side to side or rotate during the skating action. The skater's neck stays in line with the spine.

As previously mentioned, the shoulder and arm action is similar to the leg action. As the right leg glides forward, the right shoulder and arm also move forward. This shoulder and arm action rotates around the spine. This rotating action means the shoulder moves forward and the arm swings more in front of the body than to the side of the body. When manipulating the hockey stick for stickhandling, passing or pass receiving, the shoulder action is minimal. Little shoulder movement allows the skater to better control the hockey stick

Body lean is determined by speed and/or acceleration. As speed increases, so does body lean. It is important to realize that body lean must allow the leg thrust to be directed through the leg, center of gravity, upper body, neck and head. Figure 4 shows how a skater at maximum thrust has the body parts in a straight line.

This line of thrust lowers with the increased speed of the skater. Maximum angle of the line of thrust is about 45 degrees. If the upper body leans more than the 45 degrees then the upper body is bent forward too much at the hips. This results in the upper body being lower than the line of thrust. In watching a skater from the front, one will notice that the upper body and hips rotate very little, and when they rotate they rotate around the spinal column.

The Hips and Legs

The hips, like the upper body, remain relatively square to the direction of travel. The hips along with the thighs provide the power and speed to the skating action. The hips and the legs should be strong and flexible for maximum leg rotation and thrust action. Each leg uses a three phase action in the following sequence:

The Recovery Phase—after the skate makes the final thrust or push, the skate breaks contact with the ice and is brought forward under the body for the glide.

The Gliding Phase — occurs when the skate retouches the ice and glides while supporting the body.

The Pushing or Thrusting phase—is the pushing of the leg to give movement forward. Each leg moves from glide to push to recovery and coordinates itself with the movement of the other leg.

The skate in the gliding phase is pointed in the direction of travel. It supports most of the body weight and is balancing the body. The center of gravity is over this skate (figure 4). The skate passes into the push by an outward rotation of the upper leg and knee. As the push becomes stronger and more powerful, the knee continues to rotate the leg outward so that the skate can achieve more efficient ice contact and thrust.

The gliding phase leads into the thrusting phase by the outward rotation of the knee and upper leg. In the beginning stages of the thrust, the force is directed to the side of the direction of travel. As the thrust and outward rotation increase, the force becomes more in line with the direction of travel until the final stages of the toe thrust, which is almost straight ahead and in line with the direction of travel. In the gliding phase, the leg is well flexed at the knee in preparation for the long leg extension for the powerful thrust. Insufficient knee bend naturally gives an upright stride and a short inefficient thrust. Also, a skater must not shorten the glide phase. Too short a glide gives a jerky stride.

Figure 1-4: Direction of Thrust

We constantly stress the knee bend for better balance and power. Power is achieved by the straightening of the flexed leg as the skate digs into the ice. If mechanical efficiency is correct, the faster and more powerfully we can straighten the flexed leg, the faster and more powerfully we can skate.

To execute the knee bend correctly, the skater must have good ankle flexion (toes to the knees). Coaches must teach ankle flexion with the knee bend. Actually the ankle flexion should be stressed first as knee flexion depends on ankle flexion. When skaters execute knee bend with inadequate ankle flexion, they seem to skate with their upper body and rear ends behind themselves. Their center of gravity is too far back and not forward where it should be. They are the picture of imbalance.

New skates are difficult to break in because they are not built for ankle flexion. This is why new skates often hurt at the top lace area. Beginners have difficulty learning to skate because the skates prevent ankle flexion. This lack of ankle bend hampers the skater in achieving a full knee bend and as a result the beginner has a stiff straight leg stride. This straight leg stride also brings about

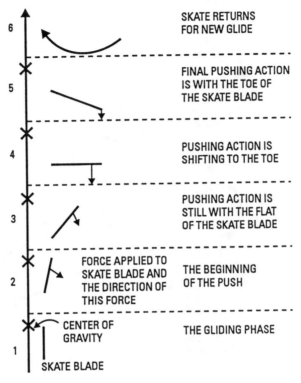

Figure 1-5: The Skating Phase

a lack of leg rotation for the maximum thrust. Also, the skater rotates his ankle outward rather than his knee and leg. This means that the skater is 'skating from the ankles' for an inefficient and weak stride.

Good skaters also do not lock the thrusting leg on the final push off before recovery. The leg becomes close to this position but not locked. Locking the leg into the full straight position causes a time consuming move into the recovery phase with no gain in power or speed. This problem also gives a jerky, weak stride.

Beginning skaters or poor skaters are readily observed when they are skating away from you. Their legs do not prescribe the circular pattern, described above, as the good skaters do.

BACKWARD SKATING

Backward skating is a demanding skill. The initial stages of learning may be difficult; however, once the technique is grasped, the skill becomes very easy and natural. The skill does require practice and lots of practice particularly for the agility requirements. Actually, very few forwards are proficient backward skaters.

Knee Bend (flexion)

Ankle Bend (flexion)

Figure 1-6: Knee and Ankle Flex

The Upper Body

The head and neck must maintain an erect position. With the head erect, the skater simply rotates the head in any direction for good visibility. Very often if the head is drooped forward, the skater must raise the head and lift the shoulders to look around. This action may temporarily create a balance problem as well as a delay when looking around. Also, if the head is drooped, the skater's body may also droop forward and give the skater an efficient body position for backward propulsion.

The arms, shoulders and upper body action is similar to that described in the forward skating action. There is a tendency to use excessive arm swinging and shoulder movement to build momentum and speed for the backward stride. This fault should be corrected as this excessive action creates time delay to the stride. Good leg thrusting action must be achieved with a minimum of upper body sway and side to side action.

The Hips and Legs

The hips must be strong and flexible. A lack of flexibility, or not using one's flexibility, forces the skater to build up speed through excessive body action of twisting from side to side. Naturally, this is not only inefficient skating, but it also makes it easier for an attacker to skate around a backward skater.

The key to the thrust in backward skating is to develop inward rotation with the knee of the thrusting leg. This inward rotation, along with proper knee and ankle flexion, puts the leg into position for a strong thrust by straightening of the leg. The thrust is as close to straight back as possible. The skate of the thrusting leg will prescribe an arc. The better skaters use a smaller arc than the poor skaters because the poorer skaters are twisting and swaying the body for momentum while the better skaters move right into the thrust back. As in forward skating, one leg is gliding while the other leg is thrusting.

Good backward skaters are able to lift the skate off the ice after the glide for a new thrust. Less efficient backward skaters do not lift the skate off the ice because of their excessive body sway and lack of excellent balance.

Some skaters skate backward by first skating forward to build up speed and then pivoting into a backward stride. An attacker can take advantage of this technique. Good backward skaters are able to build up proper speed backward using a strong initial thrusting action.

THE PIVOT

Hockey players must learn to pivot from backward to forward skating and from forward to backward skating. The main emphasis of the pivot is to lift the skate blade of the leading leg off the ice. Many skaters use the lazy style of simply twisting the skates on the ice. If there is an imperfection on the ice (a skate mark, chip, or bump) the skate blade can catch or stick into the ice and flip the skater.

Backward to Forward Pivot

In the backward to forward pivot, the skater must not cross his legs to begin the pivot. The amount of turn is governed by the amount of body and leg rotation. In figure 7, notice how the leading leg (left) is lifted off the ice and pointed in the new direction. This pivot is especially valuable to defensemen when they are skating backwards and facing their attacker, and they must pivot to maintain face to face coverage. From this position, the backward skater is able to pivot easily to the right or left by lifting and rotating the desired leg for the pivot. If the backward skater wishes to change the direction of his pivot, the leading leg simply touches the ice for a gliding action while the other leg is lifted and takes the pivot in the new direction.

Backward
skating

Left leg lifts
off the ice and
rotates with
the body to
face the
attacker. The
right leg thrusts
to the new direction.

Body is rotated;
left leg is on
the ice and
glides while
right leg takes
final thrust.

Left leg is now
thrusting in
new direction
as right leg
comes around for
it's glide.

Figure 1-7: Backward to Forward Skating

Forward to Backward Skating

This can be a little more difficult. Once again there is no crossover of the legs. The leading leg rotates inward to give a 'pigeon toed' action. The skater, while gliding forward on one leg, lifts the other leg (leading leg) off the ice and swings it around to point at the other toe. From this position the skater places the leading foot on the ice with the heel leading the glide. Timing is extremely important for the weight shift with the leg swing.

THE CROSSOVER

Skaters often use the crossover to turn and cut in a new direction. The body leans into the turn as the inside leg moves under the body. As the inside leg is pushing, the outside leg is lifting and crossing over the inside leg. The outside leg is then placed on the ice to glide in the new direction. If necessary, this crossover is repeated several times.

The crossover is acceptable in free style skating, however, once agility skating is required the crossover should be eliminated for the following reasons:

1. The crossover method does not give the skater the stability of the noncrossover method. As the leg is crossing over, the skater can easily be knocked off balance by an attacker.

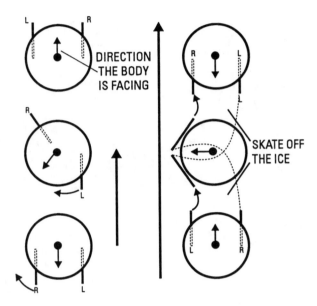

DIRECTION
THE BODY
IS FACING

SKATE OFF
THE ICE

Figure 1-8: Backward to Forward / Forward to Backward

2. Once the leg is crossing over, the skater is committed to his new direction or pivot and must complete his pivot before he can readjust. A smart attacker can use this fault to his advantage to get past the pivoting player.

3. When crossing over, the skater raises his body and straightens the inside leg. With the outside leg crossing over, the skater is leaning in the new direction. This is a weak position for stability and change of direction. The skater is unstable as only one leg is on the ice and the body is leaning to the side. Adjusting to an attacker from this position is too time consuming.

STOPS

To stop, the skater must put his skate blades at right angles to his direction of travel. In most cases it is best to use both blades, although at times one blade can be used. The stop must be executed quickly with the hips and upper legs initiating the action by rotating quickly. Failing to quickly execute the body rotation makes the stop difficult for beginners. The legs must give plenty of bend (flexion) to help in balance and shock absorption. The knee bend also lowers the body and the center of gravity to help in balance and stability. This lowering of the body by bending the knee also puts the body in position for a quick start in a new direction.

*Two-legged
stop; right leg
is bent.*

*Left leg lifts
off the ice
and rotates to
the new
direction.*

*Left leg is
placed on the
ice to glide as
right leg is
almost fully
extended.*

*Left leg glide
is now thrusting
while right leg
moves for a
thrust.*

Figure 1-9: Stop and Go

STOPS AND STARTS IN A NEW DIRECTION

The mechanics in stopping and starting in the opposite direction are similar to the pivot from backward skating to forward skating. There is no crossover. As the stop is almost complete, the inside leg is lifted and rotated in the new direction. The outside leg, bent from the stopping action, is flexed and ready to thrust in the new direction. In stopping, it is vital that the outside leg be well bent during the stop so that the leg is set for the thrusting action in the new direction.

A problem with many skaters is that their weight is on the inside leg while the outside leg goes straight. When the outside leg is straight, it lacks the thrusting action necessary for the push off in the new direction..

SCOOTING

Scooting, or scootering, is a skill similar to the action one makes on a scooter. One leg glides while the other leg provides a series of pushes. This action can be a powerful means of moving forward in close quarters or in congestion on the ice as this style of skating gives a strong and powerful base.

2

PUCK CONTROL

Puck control involves stickhandling, passing, pass receiving, and shooting. Puck control is second in importance only to the skill of skating. The skills of puck control are vital in organizing and controlling the game. Strategy is based on puck control. The team that can control the puck can control the game.

THE HOCKEY STICK

The correct lie for a hockey player will depend on his height, body lean and skating style. Although there are various methods for determining the lie and length of a hockey stick the final decision is usually on how the stick feels to the player. Trial and error will soon determine the best characteristics of a hockey stick for the individual.

STICKHANDLING

Excellent stickhandling is still in demand, despite the lack of emphasis on it by many coaches who instead stress the shooting and chasing of the puck into the end zone. The best players are usually better stickhandlers. Coaches should stress, practice, and encourage stickhandling, especially at the younger levels.

Stickhandling is a delicate art. It requires good coordination and athletic skill. The arms are held away from the body in order to provide good arm movement. Many players keep their arms too close to their body, and, as a result, their arm movement is restricted. Stickhandling should be smooth and graceful with the puck feathered back and forth in a manner much like giving and receiving your own passes. This puck manipulation must be executed in front and to either side of the body.

The puck must be controlled by feel and not eye sight. Occasional peeks at the puck may be harmless but should not be relied on. Eye sight is needed for looking around and analyzing the situation. Quite often the player has the ability to execute the skill, but he just lacks the confidence to look up and around. This lack of confidence is a fear of losing the puck. Coaches can be particularly helpful by encouraging the player to look up. Also, the coach must be careful in being too critical if the player loses the puck while stickhandling. The fear of the coach's reaction often creates fear of losing the puck in young players. During practice, some youngsters are able to stickhandle without looking at the puck, but they can't help looking at the puck in games. In this type of situation, the player just lacks game confidence in his skill. The coach should recognize this and take action in developing game confidence in the player.

PASSING

The direction of a pass is determined by two factors: the direction on the push of the stick and the angle of the stick blade. The stick must be pushed in the direction of the target and the blade must be at a right angle to the direction of the pass.

Figure 2 shows how a straight push to the target makes it easier for accuracy. In the incorrect diagram, the player moves the hockey stick blade in a circular motion around his body. For accuracy, the player must be very precise in releasing the puck. An early or late release passes the puck to either side of

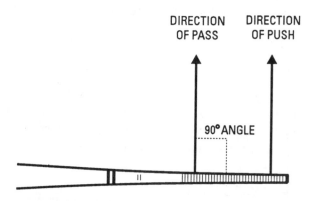

Figure 2-1: Direction of the Pass

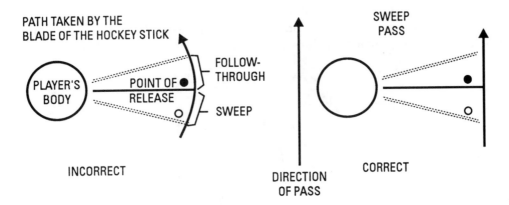

Figure 2-2: Pass Release

the target. In the correct diagram, where the stick blade is moving straight to the target, the release of the puck can be a little early or late and still be on target. Good accurate passers move the whole stick, the shaft and blade, toward the target. Poor passers have a tendency to keep the top hand on the hockey stick close to the body throughout the passing action. This helps create the circular action on the stick blade. Good passers let the top hand move with the lower hand toward the target.

In most cases, the basic pass will release the puck when the hockey stick is perpendicular to the ice and in line with the player's center of gravity. Figure 3 diagrams these characteristics. Throughout the passing action, the player must not lose his balance by falling backward or sideward. The body must stay over the pass and in balance. Proper release of the puck gives a smooth sliding pass to the target. A late release often gives a weak flipping or rolling puck. An early release is a weak, slow pass.

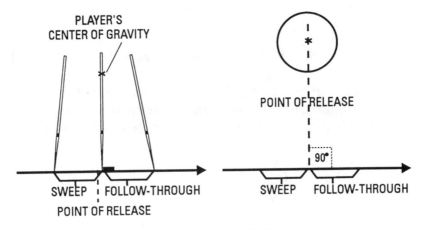

Figure 2-3: Point of Release

THE SWEEP PASS

The basic pass is the sweep pass. The mechanics have been previously discussed. The main characteristic of the sweep pass is that the blade of the stick slides along the ice for the sweep.

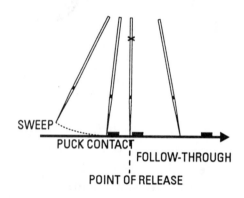

Figure 2-4: The Slap Pass

THE SLAP PASS

This is similar to the sweep pass except that the blade of the stick is off the ice for the sweep into the puck. The puck is in contact with the stick blade only when it makes contact with the puck.

THE SNAP PASS

This is like the slap pass except the sweep and follow-through are very short. The arms give the stick a short snapping action.

THE LIFT PASS

In passing, many occasions will arise when the puck will have to be lifted over an obstacle. As in figure 5, the puck is released past the center of gravity and more into the follow-through action. The height is determined by the lateness of the release. As diagramed, it is sometimes helpful to give the top hand on the hockey stick a little snap back action for extra height to the pass.

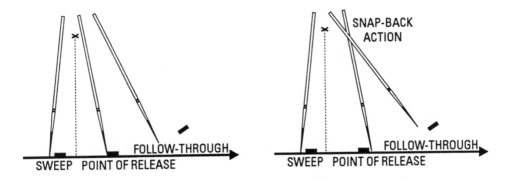

Figure 2-5: The Lift Pass

THE FLIP PASS

This is a lifting pass, except the puck is lifted to extreme heights almost perpendicular to the ice. The stick must be laid back fairly flat with the arms giving the stick a sharp push into the puck and a strong lifting action. Sometimes a little wrist snap can help.

THE BACKHAND PASS

A hockey player should be able to forehand and backhand pass efficiently to all directions. The backhand pass mechanics are similar as the forehand pass, except that the bottom hand pulls the stick for the backhand pass.

THE DROP PASS AND BACK PASS

To execute the drop pass the player stops the forward progression of the puck by placing the blade of the stick in front of the puck and holding the puck in a stationary position while the player continues to skate in his original direction. The drop pass is excellent for another player to take a quick shot.

The back pass is similar to the drop pass except the stick blade pulls the puck back to slide the puck softly backward to the intended target.

AIMING THE PASS

To pass accurately, the passer must lead the receiver. The amount of lead will depend on the speed of the receiver and the length of the pass. The passer must aim for the stick blade and not the receiver's body. It helps when the receiver puts his stick on the ice where he wants the puck.

THE BLIND PASS

This pass is not recommended in most cases, however, one can achieve success if executed at the proper time. If the passer is certain the receiver is there and no one can interfere with the pass, then such a pass can be a potent weapon.

WHEN TO PASS

An advantage of the pass is that for every good pass the opposition must make adjustments. More passes equal more adjustments by the opposition. The more adjustments a team must make the more chances there are for errors.

PASS RECEIVING

Pass receiving is just as important as passing. The two go together. If one is missing, the other is of no value.

Pass receiving requires that the blade of the hockey stick be perpendicular to the direction of the pass and that the blade gives a little to provide a cushion at puck contact. On contact with the puck, the stick blade cups a little over the puck to hold the puck down and prevent the puck from bouncing up or off the blade.

In receiving a pass, the pass receiver should place the blade of the stick on the ice where he wants the pass. With the blade on the ice, the passer has a target to aim at, and the pass receiver indicates that he is ready for the pass.

Good pass receivers are able to make adjustments to poor passes and are able to take the pass on the forehand or backhand. Such adjustments may require speeding or slowing the skating speed and drifting away or into the puck for easier pass receiving. Sometimes the pass receiver may have to release the lower hand to give more reach to the hockey stick. For passes into the feet, the good players are often able to use their skate blade to deflect the pass toward their hockey stick. Some players slide the top hand down the hockey stick to control the puck into the feet. Care must be used when looking down at the feet or behind for a pass. Looking at the feet makes a pass receiver very vulnerable to a body check.

SHOOTING

Skating and passing put the puck into scoring position. It is the shot on goal that determines a goal or just another attempt. Scoring opportunities are scarce and hard to come by so it is imperative to make the best of an opportunity.

The mechanics for shooting and passing are similar. Usually the shot is a little harder than the pass. This extra force is accomplished by spreading the hands a little further apart on the hockey stick. The shooter's weight is on the forward leg while the body maintains its forward lean and does not fall backward for the shot. The body must remain over the shot for the sweep, release and follow-through.

THE SWEEP OR WRIST SHOT

This is similar to the sweep pass. The puck is well in back of the body. The shooter's weight is on the forward gliding leg. The blade of the stick is cupped over the puck and swept forward along the ice to the point of release. The sweep begins with the arms pushing forward and downward into the ice and toward the target. At the point of release, the wrist gives a little extra snap to the shot. The follow-through determines the height of the shot. Low follow-through is a low shot and high follow-through is a high shot. The wrist snap will also determine the height of the shot. An early wrist snap gives the low shot, and a late wrist snap give a high shot.

Often when the body falls back on the shot, the center of gravity is shifted backward. This give a late wrist snap and high follow through for a high trajectory to the shot as well as a weak shot. Good shooters maintain excellent balance and keep the body lean forward.

A common problem with weak shooters is that they shoot the puck from too far in front of their body. This action gives weak arm action. Good shooters sweep the puck from well back in their stance.

Shooting in stride is a skill well worth developing. Shooting in stride is getting the shot away without altering the skating action. If the shooter can keep his legs striding, the goaltender has difficulty in reading the shot. Players who break stride telegraph the coming shot. This gives the goaltender a split second advantage. To shoot in stride, the shooter must learn to shoot off either foot. Too many players can only shoot off their strong leg.

THE SLAP SHOT

In the sweep shot, the puck is in contact with the blade of the hockey stick and on the ice for the entire sweep. In the slap shot, the blade of the hockey stick is off the ice for the sweep and makes contact with the puck just prior to the center of gravity. Figure 6 illustrates the slap shot. On the downswing, the stick is forced down into the ice and through the puck to give power to the shot.

With correct practice, the slap shot can be quite accurate. The reason for the failure in accuracy is that most players practice the slap shot for power and not accuracy. Such players usually spend hours just banging away at the puck. It would be much better to practice the power but to a target. To help in accuracy, many player find that shortening their backswing helps their control. If the shot is correctly executed the player loses very little power if any. Another advantage to the shorter backswing is that the shot is on goal much quicker. The long backswing gives the goaltender time to adjust. The shorter backswing gives the goaltender less time to react.

Puck placement can determine the height of the shot. If the puck is contacted back in the stance and behind the center of gravity, the shot will be low. If the puck is contacted forward in the stance and in front of the center of gravity, the shot will be high.

THE FLIP SHOT

The flip shot is the same as the flip pass. This shot is useful when the goalie is down and the puck must be flipped over him. The flip shot gets the puck into the air higher and quicker than any other type of shot. This shot can also be dangerous when the puck flips up into the air and lands in front of the goaltender. On landing, the puck may land on its edge and take a crazy, unpredictable bounce. Such bounces have been known to end up in the goal net.

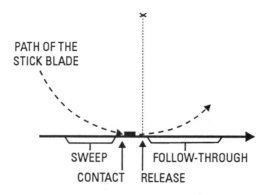

Figure 2-6: The Slap Shot

THE BACKHAND SHOT

This shot gives goaltenders problems because it is so hard to read. For this reason, it should be used more often. The backhand is a pulling action with mechanics similar to the forehand shot. A good sweep gives power to the shot. With practice, one can learn the backhand slap shot.

SHOT VARIATIONS

Under game conditions, a player is not always able to be in perfect position for the shot. This is why good shooters are able to get the shot away in or balance, in a congested or uncongested area.

PUCK PLACEMENT ON THE BLADE OF THE STICK

Some players like to shoot off the heel of the blade. Others like to shoot off the middle of the blade or the toe. Experimentation will determine which puck placement is best for you, however, good shooters are able to get the puck away off any position of the stick blade.

ACHIEVING POWER IN PASSING AND SHOOTING

Power in the shot is governed by three factors:

1. Downward force
2. Length of the sweep
3. Speed of the hands and arms.

Downward Force

When the stick is forced into the ice, the shaft is bent. This bending of the shaft causes blade lag (the blade lags behind the upper shaft of the stick). As the stick moves forward, the blade springs forward to 'catch up' with the upper part of the shaft. This catch up action increases the speed of the stick blade and, in turn, the speed of the shot. 'Catch up' speed is determined by the amount of downward force, bend of the stick, and stiffness of the shaft. The more bend, the more catch up distance, and the stiffer the shaft, the faster the stick will spring back to its original straight position. A player should select a hockey stick that will give him the best combination of these factors. Too whippy a stick will produce plenty of bend but will give slow catch up speed. Too stiff a stick will be difficult to bend and thus give little catch up distance. The player needs a stick to satisfy his style and strength. The stick must be stiff enough to provide good catch up speed but whippy enough to give good bend.

Length of Sweep

The longer the sweep, the greater the speed and momentum that can be built prior to release of the puck. It must be remembered that too long a backswing can actually be cumbersome and inefficient.

Speed of Hands and Arms

The faster the hands and arms move into and through the shot, the greater the resulting speed of the puck.

Powerful shooters are able to execute all three factors: downward force, length of sweep, and speed of hands and arms. Many, however, only utilize two of the three. Most poor shooters fail to achieve adequate downward force and as a result they have a powerless shot.

DEKING AND BEATING A CHECKER WHILE CARRYING THE PUCK

Many times during a game, a puck carrier will have to beat or get by a opponent. This deception of the opponent is known as a deke, or throwing a deke. The deke is simply a trick or deception to make the enemy think you are going to do something opposite of what you really are going to do. Such skills require good puck control and skating. When to throw the deke takes practice and experience. The deke is ineffective if executed too early or too late. The following are some common dekes and deceptions that players should work on. In many cases, the best dekes are often the simple ones that are well executed.

The Shoulder Drop: The puck carrier, on closing in on his check, drops a shoulder and gives the upper body a slight twist to the new direction. The dropping of the shoulder and the slight twist of the upper body give the impression that the skater is going in that direction. As the check moves to the new direction, the puck carrier is able to change directions.

The Crossover: The puck carrier crosses one leg in front of the other to create the impression of skating in a new direction. An opponent is often deceived into this change of direction. This crossover is a fake move from which the puck carrier can quickly recover to move in the opposite direction.

The Body Weave: The body weave is a twisting action of the body that makes the puck carrier appear to be moving in a new direction. Sometime the weave is executed several times to each side.

The Zigzag: The puck carrier approaches his opponent skating a zigzag pattern.

The Side Jump: The side jump is used to quickly evade an opponent or a body check. As a deke it can be very effective in that the puck carrier can get extremely close to the opponent and then jump to the side and regain puck possession. When the puck carrier is able to get so close to the opponent, the opponent is fooled into thinking he has the puck carrier covered.

The Draw-away: This is much the same as the side jump except that the puck carrier slips past his opponent by turning sideways and gliding on one leg.

The Change of Pace: The change of pace is the using of various speeds in sequence to deceive the checker. There are many types of change of pace and a hockey player would be advised to learn some of them. Another advantage of the change of pace is that it can be utilized with most other dekes and deceptions.

The Fast Break: The fast break is actually a change of pace, but it is so important that it can stand alone.

The Stop and Go: This is a variation of the change of pace. Instead of slowing down, the puck carrier stops and goes. This type of deke usually works best when the checker is skating along side of the puck carrier.

The Fake Pass and Fake Shot: The fake shot is especially effective on defensemen who go down to block shots. The fake pass can be effective in getting the opponent to move to an anticipated pass. Both tricks are also effective against goaltenders.

Hockey players should not become too set in their moves, dekes, and tricks, as opponents will soon learn to read them. A puck carrier with a variety of tricks is hard to read and most evasive.

3

GOALTENDING

Goaltending may well be the most highly skilled phase of the game. Goaltenders must exemplify the following characteristics:

1. Agility and coordination
2. Skating ability
3. Reflexes and eyesight
4. Hockey sense and hockey intelligence
5. Anticipation
6. Physical and mental courage

THE STANCE

A goaltender moves with explosive action in all directions. To achieve maximum efficiency for these moves, the goaltender must have a solid, strong and well balanced base. A good stance provides the necessary foundation. A poor stance with a weak base puts the goaltender in a poor position for quick moves. A weak base delays the goaltender's movement. The delay may only be a split second, but for the goaltender, a split second can be devastating.

The proper stance consists of spreading the feet and squatting with the center of gravity directly over the skate blades. The spread of the feet will depend on the goaltender's feel and style. The spread must be determined by trial and error practice to find the position from which the goaltender can make the quickest move in any direction. The squat will depend on the action around the goal: the more intense the action, the more the crouch. Whether the squat is low or high, the center of gravity or balance point must be over the center of the skate blade and between the two skates. If the balance point is in front or behind the skate blades, the goaltender will be in poor balance for moves in any direction.

It is important for the goaltender in the squat position to provide flex to his ankles, knees, and hips. The deeper the squat, the more the bend to all three joints. Lack of flexibility to either one of the joints will contribute to a weak stance. Some goaltenders have difficulty with the ankle bend. This is usually the result of the skates. The skates may be of poor design or laced too tight at the top. The ankle bend sets up the knee and hip flex for balance. In the squat position, most goaltenders will slightly knock their knees in toward each other to provide a strong position for lateral movement to either side. If the knees are bowed out or straight, the goaltender must knock the knee in for the thrust to the side. This results in slower reaction time.

The arms should hang comfortably to the side of the legs. The shoulders are loose, natural, and strong. The shoulders must not hunch or droop. The spine is fairly straight, as is the neck, so that the head is up and not drooping down. The correct stance will give the goaltender a good breathing position and will not restrict the inhale and exhale action of the lungs.

In analyzing a goaltender, check to see that he is in excellent balance and his head is up for good visibility. The stick blade is flat on the ice. The catching glove is open and facing the puck. The glove is low and ready to move up quickly. The knees are slightly turned in toward each other. Notice how this puts the skate blades in an angled position for thrusting to the side.

Also be sure that he has good ankle, knee and hip bend. The body is well balanced over the feet. The goalstick is away from the toes of the skates. This position provides a cushion for when the puck hits the stick blade. If the stick blade is tight against the toes of the skates, the puck can rebound off the stick blade into a dangerous position.

LATERAL MOVEMENT

In moving to the side (laterally), the goaltender must initiate movement by the leg farthest from the direction of travel. The action of the thrusting leg is to bend (adduct) inward at the knee and force the skate blade into the ice for a hard push. The greater the force applied, the more explosive the move sideways. Unless the knee is bent inward, the leg is unable to dig the skate blade into the ice for a strong and powerful thrust. By standing with the knees adducted, the goaltender is in the ready position for sideward movement. There is no time delay of having to adduct the knees before moving from thrusting to the side. If the resistance of one leg is taken away, the goaltender will automatically move to the side. A coach, when checking a goaltender's stance, should have the goaltender lift one leg off the ice. As soon as the leg is lifted, the goaltender should automatically be moving to that side.

THE GLIDE ACROSS

The glide across is the stand-up gliding action of the goaltender as he moves to the side to jockey for position and cut the angle. The glide across is much like backward skating with the heel leading the direction of travel. The movement is initiated by the hips and upper thighs swinging toward the direction of travel. While the hips are moving, the far leg is trusting to push the body in the desired direction. The near skate rotates to the direction of travel so that the heel leads the gliding action. The near leg also provides the balance and stability as the far leg is thrusting. While the body is gliding to the side, the shoulders, glove, and stick remain square to the puck and ready for action. The head is up and facing the puck.

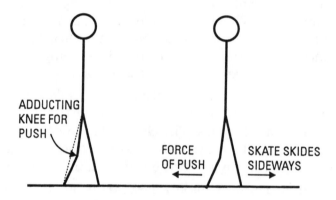

Figure 3-1: Lateral Movement

To stop the glide, the goaltender should swing his stopping leg's knee outward with the lower leg and skate following the knee until the skate blade is perpendicular to the direction of travel. As the blade moves into the perpendicular position, the leg can be forced downward so that the skate blade digs into the ice for a quick stop.

With this gliding action, the goaltender should be able to move from any spot in front of the goal to either goal post in one efficient thrust and glide. The goalie must develop an awareness of his body position in relation to the goal net. He must be able to move from his position to either goal post without looking for the goal post. The eyes must be on the puck, not where the body is moving. The goaltender's orientation of his position to the goal net must be practiced. The face-off circles, the corners, the markings on the boards all help in giving the goaltender an awareness of his position.

THE SIDE KICK

The side kick is throwing the leg out at the puck while the body remains upright. As the leg is thrown at the puck, the opposite leg thrusts into the ice to assist and speed up the thrown leg. Sometimes the thrusting leg will drop to the ice, but the body should still remain upright. If possible, it is usually best to use the stick to stop the puck along the ice. It is important to maintain balance while throwing the leg out at the puck so that the body is still ready to react in a new direction. Some goaltenders throw the leg out and then fall to the ice, off balance and out of position for any type of recovery. This must be eliminated.

THE SPRAWLING SLIDE

The sprawling slide is a very dangerous move for a goaltender. It is a diving action with the feet or the head leading. The sprawling slide is a desperation move and so the goaltender must use it as a last resort. It is acceptable if the puck is stopped and controlled by the goaltender. The big danger is that the goaltender is out of position, off balance and not ready for a rebound shot. It is very easy for the goaltender to become a "sitting duck." Very often goaltenders, when sliding out feet first, bounce their legs off the ice. With the legs bouncing off the ice, the puck can very easily slide under the goaltender's legs and into the net. Once the goaltender makes the sprawling slide, he is committed to the action, and there is no recovery. If this slide becomes common to a goalie the attackers will quickly take advantage of this by faking or tricking the goaltender into such a move.

THE ONE-KNEE SLIDE

The one-knee slide is performed by the thrusting leg's knee dropping to the ice after the thrust. The gliding leg is upright. The sliding leg must be flat on the ice and the knee should be touching the heel of the gliding leg's foot to prevent an opening between the legs. The body action is similar to a baseball player going down on one knee to block an unpredictable ground ball. An advantage of the one-knee slide is that the goaltender provides a large blocking area to the shooter. Also, the goaltender is in position to change directions quickly and efficiently. To change directions, the goaltender simply lifts the knee of the sliding leg while thrusting with the gliding leg.

THE GLOVE HAND

The glove hand is the hand wearing the catching glove. The skill of catching the puck is similar to catching a ball with a baseball glove. The goalie must watch the puck until it is caught. Taking the eyes off the puck or losing focus of the puck will result in carelessness in catching the puck. In most cases, it is best to hold the glove hand low and facing the puck. From this low position, it is easier and quicker to move the glove up than it is to move the glove lower or downward to catch the puck.

The advantage of the glove hand over the blocking glove is that the glove controls the puck by catching it so there are no rebounds or deflections. On catching the puck, the glove and puck should be brought into the front of the body, usually the chest area for protection. When moving the glove hand after the catch, it is advisable to swing the hand with a stiff wrist action. If the wrist is allowed to flip or flick, it is possible for the puck to slip out of the glove and perhaps into the net.

THE BLOCKING HAND

The blocking hand holds the goal stick and is protected by a large flat pad. The blocker, if properly used, can be valuable in deflecting shots into the corners. In most cases, the shots have to be defected because the flat surface makes it difficult to bring the puck under control, but the large surface of the blocker can make it advantageous. The weight of the goal stick and blocker can hamper speed of movement. Moving the stick and blocker should be performed by the large muscles of the upper arms and shoulders. Coaches should develop specific practice drills to improve the blocking action of goaltenders.

THE GOAL STICK

The goal stick is usually the best means of stopping shots along the ice. Sometimes the skate blade or the goal pad down on the ice is effective if the stick is out of position; however, the skate blade or goal pad does not have the control of the puck like the goal stick. The goal stick can deflect the puck at any desired angle or can cushion the puck by a little give to the stick. Cushioning the puck with the stick can leave the puck under control by the goaltender. Controlling the puck with the stick also leaves the puck in position for a pass to a teammate or a clearing shot by the goaltender. In fact, a breakout play can be effectively organized by starting with a pass by the goaltender.

In stopping shots along the ice, the goaltender must learn to slide the goal stick in either direction with the blade remaining flat on the ice. In sliding the stick to the side, it is best to keep the stick perpendicular to the ice. If the stick is allowed to lean back while moving to the side, the puck can deflect up and over the stick blade and into the goal net. It is a natural reaction for the goal stick to lean away from the shot as the stick is moved to the side. The proper movement of the goal stick is a difficult skill, but it is one that must be mastered.

THE LEGS

The goal pads are mainly used for blocking purposes. The goaltender must make the goal pads a part of him so that the pads do not impede movement and agility. Goaltenders must be physically strong to manipulate the large pads. Good goaltenders are able to deflect the puck to a desired direction. This skill must be learned to prevent rebounds from bouncing back to the opposition. Good deflection can deflect the puck to a teammate. It is also desirable for the goaltender to be able to cushion the puck on contact with the goal pads. This skill will drop the puck to the goaltender's feet so that he can pass the puck with the stick or push the puck with the skate blade to a controlled position.

THE BODY

The body is used for blocking purposes, to smother shots and protect the puck when necessary. The body should be moved behind the shot whenever possible as a means of backup protection. The body is often the main line of defense as it is used to cut down the angle of shots. The body moves forward to block out the net on the shooter. The hands, stick, and blocker look spectacular when making the save, but it is the body that positions itself to give the shooter no angle and difficulty in scoring goals. Goal net orientation and playing the angle are about having the body in position for the shots on goal.

GOAL NET ORIENTATION

In order to be in position to play the angle, the goaltender must have an excellent orientation of exactly where the goal net is while looking at the puck and not toward the goal. Goaltenders must be able to move around, side to side, forward and backward, and still be able to place their body in a position to bisect a line from the puck to the center of the goal net. A goaltender must be able to move out to cut the angle and then move back to the goalpost without looking back. Goal net orientation is a difficult skill and takes time to learn. Coaches must provide drills to help goaltenders develop this demanding skill.

To help orientation, goaltenders often use their hands and goal stick to feel for the goal post. The glove hand can be swung back quickly to feel or hit the post. The top of the goal stick shaft can be swung back to strike the goal post. The stick blade can also be used in a similar manner. Markings on the rink boards, like the angle to the blue line on the boards help in orientation by giving him a feel for his position on the ice. Very often goaltenders have difficulty when playing away from their home rink. The unfamiliarity of the rink and surroundings may give the goaltender difficulty with his orientation.

POSITIONAL PLAY OR PLAYING THE ANGLE

The goaltender must position himself in relation to the puck and the goal net. This means that the body bisects a line from the puck to the center of the goal net. On this line, the goaltender moves out or away from the net or back toward the net. It is this movement away from the goal net and back to the goal net that positions the goaltender for cutting the angle. When moving out, the goalie's body is able to block more of the net to give the shooter less net to shoot at.

Figure 2 shows a dashed line from the puck to the center of the goal net and how the goaltender moves out to cut the angle. The two solid line determine the boundary lines from the puck to the goal. The puck must remain inside these lines to hit the goal. Notice how the openings to the goal gets smaller as the goaltender moves out to the puck.

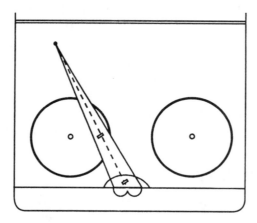

Figure 3-2

It is readily noticeable how the goaltender gives the shooter less net to shoot at by moving toward the puck. In game conditions, the goaltender must decide how far he can move out without leaving himself vulnerable behind. Naturally, the situation will determine how far from the net the goalie may move. If the goalie moves too far out then he leaves the net exposed to the non-puck carrying players to receive a pass or tip-in. Very often a goaltender will hang close to the net and then take a quick move out when he is certain the puck will be shot on goal.

Goaltenders must focus on the puck but be aware of the total play and the positioning of all attackers. This awareness will help develop anticipation of the play. This anticipation sense is difficult to develop and time consuming, but it must be practiced. Good goaltenders have learned it. Good goaltenders know that their positional play is the criteria for success. Being in position makes the play of the goal stick, the glove hand, and the blocker just that much easier. Speed of the hands and legs do not make up for poor positional play. Coaches must continually work with their goaltenders on positional play and orientation with the goal net and puck.

GENERAL RULES

A goaltender must focus on the puck but keep pace with the whole attack and the position of all the attackers. By reading the play and seeing the play develop, the goaltender will be able to make better decisions on how to analyze the play and counter the attack. When it looks like a shot is coming on the net, the goalie should study the shooter and the shooter's stick. Experience will help the goalie read the coming shot. The movement of the shooter's body and stick often give clues as to the shot or a change to a pass. Some signs of possible shots coming to the net are indicated by the shoulder and arm movement, the lifting of a leg, the head dropping for a slap shot, and a change in the skating stride. The goaltender must not only be alert to these clues but must be prepared for the fake shot, deke, or other deceptive moves.

A goaltender should remain in a stand-up position as much as possible. The stand-up position will give the best blocking area of the goal net and keep the goaltender in position to move to any new position. When it is necessary to go down, the one-knee drop is usually the most advantageous move. The one-knee drop gives good blocking area and also good position to change directions or move to a new position. Some goaltenders like the two-knee drop, and it can be effective. However, it may be difficult to get up quickly or make a recovery move from the two-knee drop position. In most cases it is best to keep the knees together with the skates apart to give the legs a little more blocking area. The two-knee drop should not be used until the skill of standing up quickly afterward is mastered. Good goalies that use the two-knee drop rock back slightly with the upper body to balance over their skates and then lift up by bringing both legs together. This skill is easier if the skates are spread and the knees are together. This is a powerful move and takes practice. Goaltenders can practice this skill without wearing the goal equipment.

The sharpness of goaltenders skates will vary with the individual and often with the condition of the ice as some ice rinks have harder or softer ice than others. The skates must be sharp enough to dig into the ice for the powerful, explosive quick moves. Dull skates cannot do the job. Goal skates should have a less hollow ground than the skates of the forwards or defensemen. Again this will vary according to the individual.

At one time, goaltenders never touched the puck unless it was to prevent a goal. Modern goaltenders now play the puck anywhere in their area. Goaltenders now control the puck behind the net and in the corners to make the pass to set up the breakout. This can be an excellent strategy as it saves time by not waiting for a teammate to skate back to get the puck. Such a delay gives the opposition time to get organized. A good pass up the rink to a teammate by the goaltender makes the attack much quicker and possibly more effective.

A goaltender must use extreme caution when the opposition has control of the puck behind the goal net. At no time must he lose sight of the puck. His body will position itself in relation to the puck. If the puck is on the left side but behind the goal, the goaltender will usually be set to the left post. When the puck moves to the right the goaltender waits until the puck is halfway across the back of the net and then he moves to the right post. If the goaltender moves too soon, the puck carrier is able to change directions and slip back around the net and put the puck into the net in the spot vacated by the goaltender.

When clearing or deflecting the puck, the goaltender should clear against the direction of the attacking or shooting player. This type of action prevents the puck from being cleared or deflected to the direction of travel of the attacker or shooter. If possible, clear and deflect to an open teammate.

TEAMMATES HELPING THE GOALTENDER

Players must be careful when falling on their goaltender to help protect the puck. Falling on the goaltender very often does not protect the puck. Instead it hampers and restricts the movements of the goaltender. Sometimes falling on the goaltender dislodges the puck into the goal net. Instead, the teammate should fall behind the goaltender to prevent a loose puck from slipping into the goal. Usually it is best to leave the goaltender alone. In the excitement of the situation, players fall on the goaltender to help him even though they do not see the puck. The goaltender's teammates should not move to help the goaltender until they are sure of their actions or see the puck so they know where and what to protect.

Teammates, especially the defensemen, must be careful when backing up toward the goal. The defensemen must shade to the side of a line from the puck to the center of the goal net. Some backup to the goal post. The main purpose is not to block the vision of the goaltender. The goaltender is playing the puck, so he must be able to see it.

Teammates must also use caution when trying to stop a shot on goal. If the shot is not fully stopped a deflection may result. Deflected shots are a nightmare to the goalie. Often the goaltender is in position or moving to position to play the puck, only to be caught off guard by a deflected puck.

GOALTENDER HELPING HIS TEAMMATES

Goaltenders should help their teammates by yelling comments. Such things like. "man behind you" or "far wing open" can be helpful to a teammate. If a teammate is blocking the vision of the goaltender, the goaltender should not hesitate to yell for him to get out of the way. Since goaltenders often have a good view of the rink and the developing patterns of play, he can often yell at his teammates as to where to pass the puck.

Goaltenders can help their teammates by stopping the puck behind the goal net. Sometimes the goaltenders can even control the puck and pass to a teammate. Goaltenders should also be ready to receive a pass from a teammate. As previously explained, goaltenders can originate the breakout play.

GOALTENDER DRILLS

In executing the drills, the goaltender must not only practice the proper execution, but he must also practice his orientation with the goal net. In the excitement of the action, it is easy to forget position and orientation. A few shots and the goaltender may end up way off line with the puck and the center of the goal. Coaches must continually monitor their goaltenders and provide opportunities for development of their positional play.

GOALTENDER DRILLS WITH NO PUCK

Post to Post: The goaltender stands at one post and moves to the other post as fast as possible. The move is performed with only one push by the thrusting leg. While the body is moving from post to post, the upper body of the goaltender should remain square to the front of the net and an imaginary puck. The head must look forward and not to the post.

From the Front of the Net and Back to Goal Post: The goaltender stands in front of the goal net, usually just outside the crease. From this position, the goaltender backs into the net to the inside of the goal post, them moves back to the spot and backs up to the inside of the other goal posts. The goaltender continuously repeats the drill. At no time does the goaltender look to where the goal posts are. The body remains facing forward throughout the drill. The goaltender should practice this drill from various spots around the goal net. As in game situations, the goaltender will have to move around from various spots in front of the net to either goal post.

From the front of the net back to the center of goal net

This is similar to the above drill, except that the goaltender moves back to the center of the goal net instead of the goal posts.

The Leg Kick: The goalie should practice kicking the leg out at an imaginary puck while maintaining balance for any recovery move. Both legs should be worked. This drill also works well with the coach or the other goaltender tossing pucks to a spot that the goaltender has to use the leg kick to deflect or stop the puck. By tossing the puck, more accuracy can be achieved in putting the puck in the correct spot for the goaltender.

The One-Knee Drop: The goalie drops to one knee and returns to his stand-up position. This is repeated several times.

The One-Knee Slide: The goaltender moves from post to post by using the one-knee slide.

The Two-Knee Drop: The goalie drops to both knees with the knees together and the feet apart. He then returns to his stand-up position in one quick move by rocking slightly backwards over the feet and straightening the legs. The hands and arms are not to be used in getting up.

Mirror Drill: The goalie imitates the actions and moves of a coach or another goaltender. Two goaltenders can take turns as leaders and use the drills as conditioners. The main emphasis of the drill is the development of the reflexes.

GOALTENDER DRILLS WITH A PUCK

Stationary Shots: Teammates line up in a semicircular pattern in front of the goal net. Have the players shoot on goal in order, and alternating sides so that the goaltender is forced to move around and work on his orientation with the net and his positional play.

Various Angle Shots: Have the players attack the net at various angles so that the goaltender can work on position play.

Lateral Movement: Have the shooter approach the goal net parallel to the goal crease line. This forces the goaltender to hug the post as the attacker is approaching and then move to the other post in timing with the attacker. This drill should be practiced with the attackers approaching from both sides.

Pressure Shots: The shooters have a contest to see how many goals they can score in a certain number of shots. The goaltender works against them to see how many he can stop. Sometimes the shooters can be divided into teams for the best record against the goaltenders. In these drills the coach can call the type of shot, like a backhand, wrist shot, slap shot, high shot, low right corner, etc.

Two-on-None: Two attackers approach the goal with no defenders except the goaltender. This situation forces the goalie to size up the situation for positional play as the attackers make the quick passes near the goal mouth.

Screen Shots, Tip-ins, Deflected Shots: If it can happen in a game, then you must practice it. Shooting drills can use a player in front of the goaltender to try and screen the goaltender. The screener can also practice his tip-ins and defecting shots.

Throwing Pucks: To work on precise movements by the goaltender it is advantageous to throw or toss the puck to certain areas of the goal. This type of accurate puck placement will give the goaltender a chance to work on or refine specific moves.

Following the Puck Behind the Net: A player carries the puck back and forth behind the goal net for an opportunity to score. The goalie must move accordingly from post to post to prevent the player from scoring.

There are many more drills and the coach can easily devise drills to meet certain situation or to work on specific moves. REMEMBER—if it can happen in a game, then practice it. Be prepared.

Section 2

Conditioning the Body and the Mind

Hockey requires excellent conditioning and fitness. The demands of the game are tremendous, and they can really take their toll on the body. Fitness must hold up over time. In the past years, only conditioning and fitness were related to the body. Now it is realized that mental conditioning is just as important as body conditioning. In fact, poor mental preparation can have a negative effect on the body. Research has even proven that athletes with mental problems, attitude problems, or stress are more susceptible to injury. Also, athletes that are stressed have difficulty conditioning their bodies. As the old expression goes, "the mind and body must work together." Unfortunately, this expression has been much talked about but little used. The modern coach must connect the mind and body — into one powerful unit.

4

Fitness and Conditioning

The training principles applied by the world class athlete and the weekend athlete are the same. The principles for conditioning the athlete are simple and easily implemented. Some books and self-appointed experts seem to feel and preach the importance of "complexity" in getting the body physically fit. If you want complexity, you can have it in your program, but you must be aware that complexity does not guarantee effectiveness. Fortunately, an effective program can be devised by following the guidelines on the principles of training. To understand our training process, we must understand the terminology.

Total Fitness: Total fitness is the term used to describe an athlete's complete fitness picture, his mental, social and physical health.

Physical Fitness: This is the health and skill area of the athlete's fitness. An athlete's health and skill level must be developed, improved, and maintained at the highest possible level from youth to retirement.

Health Aspects

Cardiorespiratory Fitness: The ability to exercise as a result of the heart, lungs, blood, and blood vessels supplying fuel, especially Oxygen to the muscles.

Strength: The amount of force accomplished by a muscle.

Muscular Endurance: The ability to use a muscle over time.

Flexibility: The mobility of the joints and the stretch quality of the muscle.

Body Fatness: The percentage of body fat.

Skill Aspects

Agility: The ability to maintain control and efficiency while the body changes positions and directions at various speeds.

Balance: Maintaining control of the body in different positions.

Coordination: The ability of the agonist and the antagonist muscles to execute movement efficiently and smoothly.

Power: The ability to perform force (strength) quickly.

Reaction Time: The ability to initiate movement quickly when needed.

Speed: Fast movement.

Overload Principle

The overload principle involves increasing the effect to increase the demands for a higher level of performance. The overload principle is the basis for strength training. In strength training, applying the overload principle means increasing the weight of the barbell so that the muscle is worked beyond its normal level. In skill learning, the overload principle is used to overlearn a skill for performance under various demands.

Progression Principle

The progression principle involves increasing the demands of the exercise as proficiency increases. In strength development, the muscle is required to exercise a weight that over time gets progressively heavier and heavier. The weight is increased to maintain the overload effect. In skill learning, the skills get more demanding and progress to higher levels from simple to complex.

Specificity Principle

The exercise must be specific to the desired outcome. Hockey is a game of quick breaks and fast speed. Conditioning the athlete must therefore be based on quick breaks and fast speed. Energy demands of goaltenders are different than the forwards, so goaltenders must be conditioned differently than the forwards. In skill learning, the style of play must be reflected in the practices. If the strategy involves a short passing game, the practice must reflect this short-passing game. Be specific. Practice exactly as you play.

Intensity: How hard? How demanding is the exercise? Intensity demands will vary, but practices must be organized to the demands of game conditions.

Frequency: How often? How many times is the drill performed? How many times a week you will practice. What are the rest periods?

Duration: How long? How long is the practice or the drill run?

Conditioning: Conditioning is the process of developing energy potential through an exercise program. This program is a physical program and is not concerned with skill development.

Training

An exercise program to develop an athlete for a particular sport or event. This program develops the athlete's energy potential (conditioning) as well as the athlete's skill level and mental abilities. Training involves the body, mind, and spirit of the athlete.

Health related fitness and skill related fitness are influenced by the principles of overload, progression, specificity, intensity, frequency and duration. The coach must manipulate these variables to produce the best possible conditioning program for each athlete and the team. Developing a program to the individual and to the team will take planning. It is not difficult; it just requires planning and understanding of the principles.

DEVELOPING A PROGRAM

Goal Setting

To develop a conditioning program, the coach must set goals. These goals are for the team and each athlete. To set goals, the coach must have knowledge of the players abilities and skills. The plans must include short term goals and long term goals.

The biggest difficulty in planning is that often the plans lack realistic objectives. On paper, coaches sometimes think they accomplish things faster than they actually do. It is best to start out with simple and easy objectives. If things go faster than expected, then there is some extra time. Also, psychologically a team may feel a sense of accomplishment as each goal is achieved. This may well be a motivational technique for a team.

Implementing a training program requires knowledge of the conditioning process as well as the game of hockey and the style of play. The coach must determine the style of play for the season and adapt the conditioning program to the demands of that style of play. This procedure meets the specificity requirement.

Interest and Motivation

An extremely important factor in designing the program is interest and motivation. Conditioning is painful and boring, but it is required and needed for any kind of team development. Plan for interest. Plan for fun. Never forget that interest and fun apply to all levels of ability — from youth league to the pros. One famous NHL hockey coach found this out when he moved from the junior A's to the NHL. The pro's and the super stars like to have fun at practice too. Humor is a strong part of the conditioning process.

Game Conditions

The training program must be demanding and as close to game conditions as possible. Practices must condition the body and the mind. The body learns to function and think under fatigue and stress. This is vital to performance. Practices must be kept moving. Dead time must be eliminated and talking must be at a minimum. Keep lectures and talk to a minimum when on the ice. Long talks are best before or after practice.

Under fatigue, athletes tend to ease up on thinking and decision making. This must not happen. Hockey games require intelligence and quick thinking. Practices must be planned for the thought process as well as the physical aspect. Sometimes it may be beneficial to fatigue the athlete at the beginning of practice and then work on complex drills and positional play to help train the athlete to think quickly and correctly while fatigued.

Overtraining and Staleness

Overtraining may well be one of the most serious problems affecting a team. It is ironic that the athlete trains hard and then reaches a stage of "too much training." No one knows where the "too much" line is. Experience seems to be the best teacher. The coach must continually look for signs of overtraining. At times, it is beneficial to ask the players how they feel.

Quite often overtraining results from guilt feelings. The coach, and sometimes the players, feel that they need a break from practice but are afraid to take a day off or cut the practice short. What makes overtraining so difficult to cope with is that each athlete experiences it individually, and they may each experience it at different times. Overtraining often leads to staleness, apathy, and a lack of excitement. The athlete is bored with the routine. The coach must plan for staleness and be ready with countermeasures when needed.

Boredom and staleness is the result of a lack of learning or a lack of progression. Planning should try to bring in new things to give variety. In athletics, we often learn everything before the season or into the early season and then practice it for the rest of the season. In the last half of the season nothing new is learned or practiced, which can make practice boring and stale.

Planning for staleness is difficult and not always possible to time, but the coach can assume as the season progresses into the later months the possibilities of staleness will increase.

The early morning pulse rate is a simple means to evaluate overtraining and staleness. Upon waking in the morning, the athlete lies peacefully in bed for a few minutes. While calm, the athlete takes his pulse. This is his basal pulse. This is done for a few days to establish the normal basal pulse. As the season progresses, the athlete should check his morning pulse before rising to see if it is at the basal rate. If the check shows the pulse to be higher than normal, the athlete may be in an overtraining state because the body is under stress and not recovering during the night's rest. If the athlete is in a state of overtraining, the coach may have to ease up on practice.

Rest

An athlete requires rest. Exercise tears the body down. Rest rebuilds the body for the new demands placed upon it. Lack of rest will gradually wear the body into an inefficient state. Fatigue becomes chronic or temporarily permanent. Prolonged fatigue is detrimental to the athlete's performance and may well require a doctor's intervention. A solitary restless night before a game is not necessarily a problem as many athletes do not sleep well on the night before competition. The problem is when an athlete suffers from fatigue for prolonged stages of days or weeks.

Sometimes too much rest is also detrimental to performance. Too much sleep puts the body in a lazy state, not only physically but mentally. Road trips are often plagued by too much sleep. The athlete sleeps-in late in the morning and then takes naps during the day because there is little to do or a lack of team activity. By game time, the athlete can be mentally foggy with slow reactions.

Pace the Conditioning Process

The coach must pace the conditioning process to the season schedule. The body needs to be sharpened for special games and rested at certain periods of the season. Planning may help to prevent athlete's from being stale or flat for important games, especially later in the season. When planning for rest, through light activity, be careful that the situation does not breed carelessness in execution. Correct skill execution must be demanded at all times.

Do not schedule heavy conditioning practices after demanding games, especially after two days of physically stressful games. When under this type of stress, the body needs rest for recovery and rebuilding of the body tissues. Practice after two days of heavy work would be best if skill development is emphasized. An athlete can maintain his level of fitness with three demanding workouts a week. Remember the body needs rest to rebuild and repair damaged body tissue. Plan accordingly. Do not panic. Do not rush the conditioning process. Panic and rushing the process puts extra stress on the body which in turn leads to injuries. Good planning will meet your objectives.

YEAR-ROUND TRAINING

Athletes must train year-round. The short preseason and season programs are not enough. Youth players may not be able to train year-round due to lack of ice, but they can be kept active in other sports and programs. At the pro and even the college level, the athletes must maintain an intensive year-round conditioning program. The off-season is the time to work on weaknesses and a strength development program. The year-round training programs used by many athletes today is one of the reasons for the longevity of the modern athlete. The athlete that goes from a lazy off-season to a demanding playing season and back to a lazy off-season is creating a tremendous strain on his body and the heart in particular. This fluctuation of on-again and off-again conditioning takes its toll in the later years of the athlete.

Strong conditioning can overcome many weakness in talent. A team's skill level decreases with an increase in fatigue. The less fatigue a team experiences during a game, the less the skill loss. Hockey is one of the most physically demanding games devised. A well-conditioned team can keep up the pressure for the entire game.

FATIGUE AND THINKING

It is a well-known fact that fatigue interferes with the thinking process. The more tired the athlete, the slower his muscular response and mental decision making. Tired athletes may not only be slow in making decisions but will often make wrong decisions.

The first sign of a tired player on the ice is not his legs but his thinking. Bad and incorrect passes, wrong positional play, and not taking a man out are all indications of poor thinking and the first sign of fatigue. A breakdown of team thinking shows a poorly conditioned team.

BODY WEIGHT

Athletes should maintain proper playing weight. There are charts and methods to determine body fat on a individual; however, simply looking at the athlete can often reveal an overweight or underweight problem. Very often an underweight problem is associated with a lack of interest, excitement and energy. The eyes may even show a dullness. Many teams record their weight daily. This is a good way to detect weight deviations as a weight increase or decrease can signal a problem. Consistent loss or gains may well require a doctor's checkup, so be alert.

WARM-UPS AND STRETCHING

Stretching should not be done without a good warm-up. A problem with stretching exercises is that athletes do them as a means of warming up. Runners will stretch before they run as a means of warming up the body for the stress of competition. Stretching is no longer recommended as a warm-up. Stretching the cold muscles often result in minor and minute tears to the muscles, tendons, and sheath covering of the muscles. Under the intense stress of competition these tears increase and eventually become serious injuries later in the competition or even weeks later. Warm-up then stretch.

WATER

Athletes must drink water to meets their thirst and body needs. Many experts now even recommend extra water before competition and before the thirst develops. Water is mandatory for performance as performance deteriorates in the later stages of the game if the body lacks water.

HEAT

As heat increases, sweat increases and so does the need for water. Hot arenas create this problem. Dry land conditioning may be more of a problem if the day is hot and humid. Heat makes the athlete sweat more, and the humidity prevents the sweat from evaporating and hinders the cooling process. If exercising outdoors, care must be taken. A hat is often a preventive measure to the sun's rays. Do not wear rubber or plastic material to cause the body to sweat and lose weight. This technique does not cause loss of body mass. It only means a loss of water weight. This weight loss will soon be gained back when the athlete drinks any liquid or eats food. Wearing of plastic or rubber suits puts the body in or very close to dehydration by increasing the sweating of the athlete. Dehydration can be extremely dangerous.

If at any time an athlete feels nausea, dizziness, or disorientation while exercising, dehydration may be the cause. If dehydration is suspected, cool the body fast.

AEROBIC ENDURANCE AND ANAEROBIC POWER

Understanding the energy systems of the body can be complex; however, for our purposes, we will discuss the aerobic and anaerobic factors as simply as possible.

The human body requires carbohydrates, fats, and proteins as fuels for energy. Of these three fuels, carbohydrates are the main energy source. Fats are the secondary source for energy, and proteins are utilized only when carbohydrates and fats are not present. These three nutrients provide the fuels for energy the body needs. This is why nutrition is so important to the athlete. Food is broken down by the body to form glucose or simple sugars. The glucose is stored in the muscles and blood for energy on demand. The extra glucose is stored in the liver in the form of glycogen as a reserve for when the muscles and blood run out of glucose. The breakdown of glucose for energy is the result of a process called glycolysis. The glycolysis process functions in two ways - a "fast glycolysis" and a "slow glycolysis." The fast glycolysis is termed anaerobic and the slow glycolysis is termed aerobic. Aerobic means "air" or containing oxygen. Anaerobic means no oxygen or air as "an" means "no" or "not".

FAST AND SLOW GLYCOLYSIS

The fast glycolysis (anaerobic) is utilized for quick, demanding powerful short bursts of energy. If the energy is required quickly, the anaerobic system will meet the body's demands. The sugar or energy in the muscles and blood is immediately utilized without the benefit of oxygen. Since the supply of glucose in the muscles and blood is limited, the time span for this system is short and rarely can go beyond one minute under maximum demands. The anaerobic system is under maximum use for short quick breaks, pushing in the corners, line shifts, etc. The one hundred yard dash is the classic example of anaerobic energy system.

The slow glycolysis (aerobic) is used for less demanding activity and for energetic activity over a minute. When the activity is slower, as when the player is coasting or comfortably skating, the oxygen taken into the body is utilized to sustain the glycolysis process over time. Marathon runners utilize the aerobic system as the oxygen maintains the energy needed for the run.

ENERGY SYSTEMS FOR ICE HOCKEY

Ice hockey demands both systems. The quick break requires the anaerobic system, and the coasting or pacing of the speed brings in the aerobic system. After a quick break or a sustained period of high intensity effort, the body slows down with excessive heavy breathing. This heavy breathing is putting oxygen back into the system to maintain the glycolysis for replenishing the body energy needs. The body needs oxygen for energy. On quick breaks, the immediate energy is depleted. Heavy breathing after the quick break or shift is needed to put oxygen back into the system to reenergize the body.

Hockey is a fast and demanding game. The players are rotated or shifted on and off the ice after about a minute of activity. Sometimes, if the demands are not too strenuous, the players may stay out a few seconds longer than the minute. Too long a shift can become a dangerous situation because maximum anaerobic efficiency lasts only about a minute. Go over this minute, and the player may run out of energy before his shift is over. A coach should not expect a player to gain his energy back while on the ice especially if the player has given full effort to his shift. If the anaerobic system is used for the minute or close to the minute, the body is under fatigue and it requires heavy breathing to regain energy.

When an athlete skates at full effort for a minute using anaerobic energy, lactic acid or fatigue acid is built up as a result of the lack of oxygen. Heavy breathing helps to reduce this lactic acid build up for the next shift. As the athlete's body becomes physically fit and in peak condition, the lactic acid build up is lessened and the lactic acid is cleared quicker and more efficiently.

The coach should develop a strong aerobic base conditioning program in the preseason and early season. As the season gets underway, the program should slowly develop the anaerobic system through interval training. In developing the interval program, the ratio factor is imperative to maintain game conditions. The rest phase of the interval is needed to recharge the athlete for another maximum anaerobic effort. A conditioning program that fails to meet game ratio requirements will fail to recharge the athlete when he sitting on the bench waiting for his next shift. Fatigue will set in for the later stages of the game.

DRY LAND PROGRAMS

Many teams are using dry land conditioning in the off and preseason until the ice is ready. Such a program is valuable to the athlete in not only the physical conditioning but the mental aspects of preparing for the season. A good dry land program should not only contain traditional running exercises and drills but should also emphasize various aspects of running. The following are examples of various exercises.

Fast Breaks: Fast breaks should be practiced from a dead stop and from a slow run and from half-speed runs. The athlete should alternate starting legs so that the athlete does not become dependent on always starting with the same leg. It is amazing how many hockey players have a preference on a certain leg for starts. If they are in a situation where they must start with their weak starting leg their start is weak because the weak leg does a weak push in order to get the strong starting leg in position. Develop both legs equally so that an efficient start can be made with either leg.

Hopping: The hockey player should practice hopping with each leg and with both legs together. Hopping is good for increasing the work load of the legs and for increasing agility.

Backward and Sideways Running: Backward running provide athletes with an opportunity to develop different muscles than those developed by running forward. Backward and sideways running are also an excellent means for developing agility.

Jogging: Various speeds for different results. Excellent for warm-ups and cool-downs. Also, good for recovery between exercises like fast breaks, hopping, backward running, etc.

GAMES AND SPORTS

Various team and individual sports are an excellent means to condition an athlete. They are fun and exciting. Doing drills certainly gets boring and many of the players will perform the drills as a routine practice. Games will create a competitive atmosphere with the players giving an all out effort. Motivation for the games is usually high. The games should be played at a fast pace. If necessary, change the rules to keep the game moving.

Team sports: Basketball, field hockey, soccer, speedball, team handball and volleyball.

Individual sports: Badminton, bicycling, karate, racquetball, handball, swimming, table tennis and tennis.

DEVELOPING MUSCULAR STRENGTH AND MUSCULAR ENDURANCE

Weight training is designed to strengthen the body for explosive effort as well as sustained muscular effort. It is important to remember that weight training does not develop cardiorespiratory endurance. Weight training develops muscular strength and endurance of the muscles only. Cardiorespiratory endurance is developed through the aerobic system.

Devising a weight training program is relatively easy. Simply follow the conditioning guidelines and principles. Extensive and complex programs are available from the many books out in the market. If the coach desires more information on strength training, then extra outside reading could be helpful. Two books published by Masters Press are especially good. They are *Kinesiology of Exercise* by Michael Yessis, copyright 1991 and *A Practical Approach to Strength Training* by Matt Brzycki, copyright 1991.

Many books and articles will prescribe a certain program for hockey players. Such programs place emphasis on certain body parts like the wrists for shooting. Placing too much emphasis on certain body parts actually overdevelops these parts of the body. Such overdeveloped parts or muscles put an extra strain or stress on the other muscles to make them more prone to injury. A proper program will develop all the body parts equally to put the body parts in balance.

NUTRITION

This area can be covered by an entire book. We will break it down as simply as possible.

An athlete needs a well balanced diet. This requirement is as simple as eating a little of all the good foods. This policy will usually provide the necessary requirement.

Simple Guidelines

- Eat a variety of foods.
- Eat plenty of vegetables, fruits and grain products.
- Maintain a diet low in fat, saturated fat, and cholesterol.
- Sugar, salt and sodium should be minimal.
- Maintain proper weight.

Pregame and Postgame Meals

The pregame meal is not as important as a proper daily diet. One meal before the game will not solve daily problems in lack of nutrients. The pregame meal should be comfortable to the athlete. Fatty foods and fried foods should be eliminated and condiments, sauces and salts should be kept to a minimum. Easily digestible foods that are high in carbohydrates are best.

The postgame meal should also be high in carbohydrates with perhaps adequate meat for proteins for tissue repair, although a proper daily diet should not leave the athlete in demand for proteins after a game.

5

MENTAL CONDITIONING

The previous chapter discusses the physical conditioning aspect of the athlete. However, the physical aspect of training the body is only half the job. Today's athlete must be conditioned not only physically but mentally; both are of equal importance to the total being of the athlete. More and more the experts are realizing that the mind controls the body, as scientific facts are continually being discovered to support and strengthen this conviction.

MENTAL PRACTICE

Today the modern coach must think in terms of mental practice coordinated with physical practice. For some reason, coaches and athletes perform physical practice until game time and then expect their mental skills to take them to new heights. The pregame pep talk was believed to be the criteria for mental preparation. To be beneficial, the mental practice of psychological skills must be practiced along with the physical workout throughout the season. This is realistic as game competition requires both the mental and physical attention of the athlete. At the end of a workout, the athlete's mind must be tired along with the body.

In order for the human body to perform at its maximum ability, the body must be physically trained over a period of time. This training principle must also be applied to psychological skills. Psychological strategies must also be practiced and refined over time in a way similar to physical practice. Since we do not go into a game and expect an athlete to perform a skill without the proper physical preparation, we should not expect an athlete to go into a game without the proper mental practice.

Coaches and athletes read about psychological skills and conclude that they already do it or that it is too easy to be effective. Well, mental skills are easy to learn and practice when there are no distractions or pressures, but when distractions are present, those skills may be very hard to execute. Game pressures, fatigue, excitement of the situation, fear of failure and other fears and distractions all have an effect on the athlete's thinking. These distractions interfere with the thought process and prevent the desired focus of attention and concentration. Thought stopping is an extremely easy psychological skill to perform in pressureless situations, but, under pressure, many athletes are unable to execute this mental skill. Distractions interfere with their focus. Often this lack of ability to perform thought stopping is simply a lack of practice and a knowledge of the skill. Game condition practices must be provided so that the athlete has an opportunity to practice the necessary psychological skills. This is why it is important for the coach to develop practices with game situations and pressures.

SKILL LEARNING

Skill learning involves three stages:

1. Understanding
2. Practice and error correction
3. Automation

The understanding stage is a thinking stage in which the learner develops a knowledge and feel of the skill. The second stage of learning requires practice and error correction. This is the longest and most demanding stage. The learner is in a trial and error process. Feedback is essential for error correction. The more effective the feedback, the more productive the learning situation. Without feedback, learning is practically nonexistent. If a player does not know how he is performing, then he has no basis for changing behavior. If the player does change behavior with no knowledge of results, then there is no assurance that it is for the better. As a skill improves, the learner progresses towards the ultimate stage of automation. In the automation stage, the skill is executed automatically and in a reflexive manner. No analysis of movement is required.

Imagery and Skill Learning

Imagery can play an important role in all three stages of skill learning. In the understanding stage, the learner uses 'concept imagery' by focusing on the whole skill to develop a complete concept. This can be done through the use of movies, video, still pictures, or by watching the better performers. It is important at this stage of learning to see good execution so that the correct imagery sets the pattern for future development.

In the practice and error correction stage, 'execution imagery' focuses on the body movements and the execution of the skill. Imagery can be particularly helpful in this stage of learning by providing feedback. By visualizing the correct body movements, the body's musculature system acquires feedback for the correct skill execution.

To reach the automatic stage, the athlete must progress from focusing on body movements to focusing on the desired results or outcome of the skill. This desired result or outcome type of focus is called 'outcome imagery' or visualization. The golfer visualizes the flight of the ball and not the body movements for striking the ball. The bowler focuses on the roll of the ball and not the body movements for rolling the ball. The baseball pitcher uses imagery to visualize the ball curving into the strike zone and does not visualize the body movements for throwing the curve ball. The hockey player looks at the open area of the goal net and shoots for the opening with no thought as to how to shoot the puck.

The practice phase must be used as a means of preparation for the automatic stage. The use of 'execution imagery' to improve body movements must give way to 'outcome imagery' once the execution of body movements are fairly proficient. If too much practice and time is spent on 'execution imagery' then the athlete may become so ingrained with body movement imagery that the athlete cannot make the transition from execution imagery to outcome imagery and visualization.

LEARN LIKE A KID

When learning a skill, kids are on a trial and error process. They try, and if it doesn't work, they try again. Very little coaching is involved or needed. The kid attacks skill learning with wild abandon and enjoyment. They 'fool around' with different ways to perform a skill like throwing or hitting a ball. They experiment. As they fool around and experiment, they learn a feel for the skill. A feel of control, balance and body manipulations that fit each individuals musculature and bone structure. The child does not become paralyzed by analysis.

Adults must try to learn skills like a kid. They must focus on feel. The mind must be clear with a simple single focus. Often, adults become so serious that they forget to have fun and enjoy the learning process. Fun and enjoyment help to cope with the frustrations of learning. Be a kid and have fun, experiment, and free wheel your movements.

KEEP IT SIMPLE

Modern technology, like high speed photography, video taping and research has developed a wealth of technical information on skill technique and skill execution. This information is valuable; however, coaches must not overuse this information and fall into the over-coaching syndrome. As coaches, we must glean this technical information and present it to our athletes in a simple manner, organized and with a logical learning progression. Many coaches are so technique oriented that they prevent the athlete from developing a natural feeling for a skill. Some coaches confuse the athlete's mind with too many technical facts. This stimulus overload of information confuses the mind and prevents a strong focus of attention.

AS A COACH, DISPLAY CONFIDENCE IN YOUR PLAYERS

A coach must not let a little failure destroy an atmosphere of confidence and determination. The coach must not display a quitting attitude or convey an attitude that he has given up on his players. When things are bad, coaches should continue to show confidence. Sometimes a pat on the back and encouragement tells the players that the coach still has faith in them.

Motivation

Coaches are constantly evaluated by their ability to motivate. This evaluation seems to generate an atmosphere on motivation being the coach's responsibility. Maybe in some ways it is, but motivation is the athlete's responsibility too.

Despite the coaches preparations, when it comes to the final test it is the athlete who must rise to the occasion. It is the responsibility of the athlete to excite himself to the level of motivation necessary to execute the slap shot, bodycheck the opponent in the corner, or skate to a high pain level. "You can lead a horse to water but you cannot make him drink." The coach-athlete relationship is of similar philosophy. The coach can prepare the athlete, and lead him to the game, but it is the athlete who must drink the water of performance.

Athletes must take responsibility for their motivation. Coaches can help, but coaches are not solely responsible. If an athlete lacks motivation then the coach must take serious steps to solve the problem.

Post Playing Depression

"During my two year recovery from a near fatal auto accident, I found I was able to cope with the medical treatments and physical adjustments. The traumatic aspect of my new life style was not the absence of playing hockey but the psychological aspect of not being the center of attention and the accompanying loss of identity. I could not adjust to being an ordinary person." This quote came from a college hockey player. When an athlete is no longer able to play his/her sport for whatever reason, the problem is not the lack of playing but the loss of identity. The athlete no longer feels the adulation and the sense of being special. The feeling is like being pushed into obscurity. The camaraderie of the group is gone.

Loren Coleman, a researcher at the University of Southern Maine wrote a book called "Suicide Clusters". An interesting aspect of this book is the high rate of suicides among Major League baseball players after they have left the game. A player makes the Majors, he is part of "America's favorite pastime" and has cards printed up with his picture in the hands of fans everywhere and then he is forced out of the game by an injury, a bad season, or he simply retires. The player's career ends and he has no safety net, no way of coping with life outside of sports. Coleman stresses the need for a counseling program to help the players adjust to retirement.

Careful analysis of this post playing depression syndrome is not just with professional athletes. College, high school and youth players also suffer from this depression syndrome. High school stars familiar to their special status in high school also suffer when they fail to make the college team. Youth programs also find kids who suffer from being cut or failing to succeed when playing. Post playing depression is at all levels.

Although the coach has many responsibilities and very little time, the coach must find ways to help players who are cut, dropped, or retired feel good about themselves even when not participating. It is difficult, but we must be aware of this serious problem.

Psychological Strategies

Although the use of psychological strategies are helpful, it is important to understand that no psychological technique can be employed that will make an athlete perform better than his physical skill ability. Psychological strategies can only help to bring out the maximum physical skills of an individual. A high level of performance requires a high level of skill. This is a fact that must never be overlooked. Psychology will not make up for a lack of skill.

There are, however, many athletes who are not achieving their maximum potential because their mental skills are lacking. Often, we see the player with amazing skating efficiency and speed, but his thinking cannot keep up with his speed. Under physical effort, some players' thinking ability deteriorates. Many athletes can improve their performance simply by using psychological strategies to create a mental atmosphere that will let their body perform their physical skills to the best of their ability.

Mental strategies may not do wonders the first time out on the ice. There will be ups and downs and times when the coach and the players are convinced that mental skills do not work. The psychological skills outlined in this book do work and are very effective. Like physical skills, mental skills must be practiced. Fortunately, learning and practicing the mental skills are simple, very simple, and actually take very little time. Practice will soon bring beneficial results.

There are two basic situations for using psychological strategies. One of the situations is when actually performing, **The Performance Phase**, and the other is when not playing but preparing for the game/season, **The Preparation Phase**. The preparation phase involves setting goals determined by an assessment of your needs and abilities. This is the phase for developing the mental skills of relaxation, imagery and visualization. It is also the time for fine tuning coping strategies that will help the player cope with anxiety, fear, confidence, etc. The performance phase uses quick recall strategies that can be strengthened through the preparation phase practice. The performance strategies will be discussed first as they can be readily applied to the next hockey game.

THE PERFORMANCE PHASE: Psychological Strategies for Use While Performing

While reading the following strategies, do not believe that these strategies are two simple to be effective, or that you already employ such strategy. If you feel that you already are using such a strategy, then make an honest appraisal as to how effective it is. Psychological strategies applied in a careless manner will be more hazardous than if not applied at all. Carelessly applied mental strategies send incorrect or confused messages to the muscles. Incorrect mental messages will result in incorrect muscular movements. Confused mental messages will give the muscles confusing and uncertain directions. Simple mental strategies are often more effective than complex strategies because the simple strategies are easier to develop and send clear, accurate messages to the muscles. The following strategies must be practiced and practiced correctly until you are able to utilize them automatically.

Thought Stopping

The effectiveness of this technique lies in its simplicity and ease of application. Most athletes use it. Some athletes are even unaware that they do use it. Whenever the mind is not settled or is confused, simply stop the thinking/feeling process and reorganize your thoughts. Hockey is a fast moving game with little or no time for thinking as most of the moves are reflexive and automatic. Despite this fast moving pace, the athlete must still practice thought stopping while playing. When the mind is frustrated, the player must control it by stopping the frustrating thoughts and thinking in a new direction. If the mind is confused, the player must stop the confusing thoughts and reorganize. With so much of the game played in automatic or reflexive mode, it is very difficult to counter with change of thoughts; however, it can be done with practice.

A hockey player must do an honest evaluation of his problems and determine what to work on. When this is done, the athlete can decide on priorities. It is best not to try and work on too much at one time. Take priority number one and practice it during games and practices. As improvement develops then another priority can be added. Do not panic and rush the process. Be thorough.

Self-talk

Self-talk can be effective in lowering anxiety, confusion, and fears. Self-talk should be positive. The idea of recalling past successful experiences is important in developing a positive attitude. Past successful experiences develop positive successful pictures in the mind. Negative talk may develop negative and destructive pictures in the mind. Negative pictures of past failures or even possible future failures help reinforce the mind for failure. Negative self-talk can also increase pressure and raise the anxiety level of the athlete.

If interest or motivation is low then stimulating self-talk can be used to stimulate the body and mind to perform better. This type of self-talk is used to help prevent carelessness in thinking. One must be careful not to turn stimulating self-talk into pressure self-talk. An example of stimulating self-talk would be, "Stay alert, only four minutes left. Concentrate. Stay energetic. I must play my game. I will continue to play aggressively." Pressure self-talk for the same situation would be, "If I don't concentrate they are going to score. Then I am in trouble. I cannot lose this game. We must win."

Self-talk must be within the physical abilities of the talker. Remember, you cannot talk yourself into executing skills beyond your capabilities. To be effective, self-talk must be positive and realistic.

Rational Thinking

Rational thinking coincides with self-talk and positive thinking. Rational thinking must be realistic as the thinking must be to the capabilities of the hockey player. Many players destroy themselves by feeling that every skill or shift must be perfect. Every shift cannot be perfect and some errors will occur. Good shifts may have errors from time to time. It is useless to worry over the errors when the play is over. All that can be done is to learn from the mistakes for the future. The distinguishing feature of good athletes is their ability to make comebacks after the bad play. The good players are mentally tough.

Rational thinking will help turn defeat/mistakes into a learning situation. A player must learn from mistakes, otherwise there is little chance for improvement. Mistakes will occur, so the player must learn to accept this fact and continue to perform without worrying about past mistakes.

False Assumptions

Another important aspect of rational thinking is to not make false assumptions. False assumptions are thoughts beyond one's abilities. An example of a false assumption is when the puck carrier tells himself that he can beat the two defensemen and score instead of passing the puck.

Positive Thinking

Positive thinking is most helpful if it is regulated by rational thinking. No matter how positive one is, it is essential to have the skill to achieve the positive thoughts. Positive thinking is not a cure-all or a cover-up for mistakes. Positive thinking is intelligent analytical thinking with no foolish reasoning or wishes.

Some players confuse positive thinking with wishful thinking. Remember—hockey is not a fantasy game. The hockey player is in a real world requiring correct thinking and execution. Hoping or wishing will not achieve the objective. Positive thinking should be a part of your self-talk and rational thinking skills, but it must be realistic to be effective.

Successful results through positive thinking reinforces a positive attitude; however, positive thinking can easily turn into negative reinforcement. Using positive thinking to attempt skills beyond one's ability may lead to many unsuccessful performances. These unsuccessful attempts may well develop a lack of confidence and a negative approach to executing skills of a similar nature. To prevent a possible negative approach to positive thinking, it is important that the athlete knows his skill level, capabilities and limitations. It is of little value to think positively when executing a skill beyond one's ability. Successful performance requires positive thoughts being in harmony with one's skill level. As a physical skill improves so does a player's confidence and, in turn, a player's positive approach.

Lessening the Importance of the Situation

Pressure increases with the importance of the situation. As pressure increases, tension may also build in the body. Some athletes, in order to cope with anxiety and tension, convince themselves that the situation is not as important as they believe. Sometimes this can be effective. The big problem with this technique is that if the player convinces himself that the situation is not important then an informal, lazy, or even a careless attitude may be created. Such a careless attitude may well develop into a careless performance. A goaltender that feels that an easy shot is not important may become careless in the execution of stopping the puck and suffer drastic consequences of letting in an easy, stupid goal.

Perceptions

Perceptions are the big psychological factor in controlling anxiety and tension. How we perceive the situation may be vital to our anxiety and muscular tension control. Good athletes perceive a game situation as within their capabilities. Poor athletes perceive the same situation with uncertainty or as too much to handle. Good athletes realize that pressure is what they put on themselves as a result of their perception of the situation. They are good because they know how to handle such situations. They have been there before and their past experiences have taught them how to cope.

Athletes have different perceptions of the same situation. Penalty killing is perceived as fun by some or a threat by others. Some players fear killing a penalty, as the chances for a goal is increased. Such a goal is a threat to their ego, a reflection of their ability. Some players love the challenge of preventing a goal while the odds are against them. Some players feel a goal against them while killing a penalty means little because the odds are for a goal anyway.

Negative perceptions of a situation can be improved by mental and physical practice. Mental strategies will help to perceive the situation as less threatening. Physical practice will help to develop successful recall, reinforcement, and the positive attitude and thinking that comes from successful skill execution. As practice develops better skills, negative perceptions will slowly disappear as positive perceptions increases. Imagery can help one perceive a situation as less threatening. This technique will be discussed later in the preparation phase.

Mental Recall

One's perception of a situation is usually based on one's past experiences. For this reason, the hockey player should develop a backlog of successful experiences. From this backlog, the player can recall the successful past experience needed for the present situation. This recalling of successful past experiences can reinforce a positive attitude, confidence, positive self-talk and a good mental image for coping with the situation.

Confidence

Confidence is not a result of positive or rational thinking, nor is it a result of some one telling a player how good he is. Confidence is the result of thorough knowledge of one's abilities for the situation at hand. Confidence can be situation specific; a player may be confident with a wrist shot and yet be lacking in confidence for the slap shot. A player may have hockey playing confidence but a strong fear as a dinner speaker.

Confidence is gained through successful past experiences. Practice and experience build true confidence. False confidence is an exaggerated belief in one's abilities. False assumptions are part of false confidence. Successful skill execution is needed to convince the mind that one is capable of performing the skill. As a skill improves, the mind becomes more convinced of the body's ability to perform the skill and so the confidence of the athlete is also able to improve.

THE PREPARATION PHASE: Psychological Strategies for Use When Not Performing

The psychological strategies discussed here are practiced when not playing. These strategies require a little more time and preparation than the previously discussed strategies. However, the time spent is well worth it. In simple terms, the hockey player is using mental exercises to train the muscles to perform physical skills correctly.

At present, there are numerous mental strategies to help a hockey player. Some strategies focus on the development of correct skill execution. Some strategies focus on the control of tension and anxiety. Other strategies focus on various positive factors like confidence, self-talk, rational and positive thinking. Various researchers have developed their own mental strategy programs and there are many of them on the market and in books and articles. Research has proven that they all work. As to which is best, it would naturally depend on individual and situational needs. It is interesting to note, that almost all these mental strategy programs involve the skills of relaxation and imagery. Since most programs are basically similar, this book will outline its own mental strategy program that is adaptable to specific needs of the athlete. Our program involves the following phases:

1. Goal setting
2. Physical and mental skills assessment
3. Relaxation
4. Imagery
5. Evaluation

Goal Setting

Before developing a mental practice program, it is best to assess the situation as to where improvement is needed. This assessment is in the form of goal setting. You must analyze your play to determine where mental practice is needed and what goals or objectives will meet this need. It is important to keep the goals realistic. A big problem in goal setting is that most people set goals that are too high. High goals are not to be eliminated, but high goals should be achieved in stages. Start off simply, achieve smaller goals and then reset your goals to a higher level. Work your way up the ladder. Start off too high and you may become discouraged by realizing that you are not meeting your objectives.

Assessment

The coach and the players decide what skills need development. Physical skill can be helped with mental practice in the form of imagery. The players' mental coping strategies like anxiety, fear of the corners, confusion, confidence, etc. can also be helped through imagery. Imagery practice is performed while the body is in a relaxed state. Relaxing the body is usually done through imagery and self-talk.

Relaxing the Body

To practice relaxation techniques, select a comfortable position in a chair, recliner, bed or flat platform. Close your eyes and prepare your body for the relaxed state. Think relaxation. Picture yourself relaxed. Focus your attention on your breathing. Breath in a relaxed and controlled manner. Keep it even and rhythmical with equal time on inhalation and exhalation. Sometimes a picture of yourself floating on a cloud may help. With each exhalation, feel yourself getting more relaxed with tension leaving the body with each breath. As the body becomes relaxed, feel the body becoming warmer and more comfortable. As the body goes more and more into a relaxed state, focus your attention on specific parts of the body and use self-talk to increase your awareness of relaxation to the body part.

Imagery

Brainwaves occur in two major wave lengths. They are ALPHA, the fully relaxed state and BETA, the more active or fully awake/alert state. Imagery should be practiced in both states.

Imagery is an effective technique, providing that you keep it simple, vivid and accurate. Like goal setting, you must work from the simple to the difficult. From your assessments, you can easily determine your order of priorities. Imagery is used to help cope with skill development and mental development.

Imagery for skill development

As an example of skill development through imagery, we will use imagery to develop the skill of shooting in stride. Shooting in stride is an excellent skill to have. Goaltenders have difficulty reading the shot as the skating action of the shooter does not alter for the shot. Also, the shot is released much quicker if the player does not have to adjust his feet for the release of the shot.

In the relaxed state, the athlete focuses on the skill of shooting in stride. A clear picture is developed in the mind of executing the skill perfectly with the legs in various positions and the body balanced. Do not rush the process. Go slow and easy. Get the picture and let it burn in the mind. Go from picture to picture slowly.

The mental practice of the skill must be followed with physical practice. When on the ice, bring up your picture and execute. This technique combines the physical and mental practice for the best learning technique.

Imagery for Mental Development

Imagery for mental development is performed in much the same way as for skill development. An example of mental development imagery would be the control of fear/anxiety for the corners. When the body is relaxed then focus on play in the corners. Develop a clear and vivid picture of yourself skating in the corner at full speed and taking out a player and getting the puck. Various situations can be worked on. Imagery of taking out two players in the corner and different spacing of the players will help to develop various plans of attack.

Imagery can also be used for controlling other problems, like player anger and frustration. While in the relaxed state, the athlete pictures situations that make him mad. With each of these situations, the athlete pictures himself tolerating the situation and coping with it in a controlled and cool manner. The image of "supercool" is developed in the mind. In games and practice, an anger situation should trigger the picture of the correct response of supercool.

Anxiety and tension problems can also be attacked with this type of imagery. It is important that you do not use a negative statement for your picture or imagery development. Imagery is thinking with pictures and the mind cannot see a negative picture. If you develop your image with self-talk like "don't miss the goal net on the backhand", then the mind develops the picture of the puck going wide of the goal net. The body reacts to this picture. Keep the pictures positive. Develop the picture of the puck going into the net.

Imagery should be practiced when we put our body in a relaxed state. Practice in this alpha (relaxed) state is for developing muscle memory in coordination with the mind. Imagery should also be practiced while not in the totally relaxed state but in the beta (active) state. In the beta state, imagery can be practiced for a few short minutes, or even seconds, while behind the desk at work, during a commercial break on television, or while waiting for a bus. Imagery practice in the totally relaxed alpha state will assist the imagery practice in the beta state. Imagery practice in the beta state is also helpful in developing the use of imagery for playing conditions.

Imagery used while performing is called visualization. Most professionals use visualization of the shot on goal before execution even though they may not formally practice imagery. The shooter looks at the goal or target and shoots the puck at the target. There is no imagery on the body mechanics. Children use a lot of imagery and visualization when they are learning and playing sports. They often dream of their performances in the big time. Many children play imagery or fantasy games against the top professionals and see themselves scoring the winning goal for the Stanley Cup. As adults, most people would be so much the better if they incorporated their childhood dreams into their development and learning situations.

Evaluation

All practice sessions, physical and mental, should be evaluated. If necessary keep records to help evaluate performance. If results are not developing then check techniques and procedures.

OTHER MIND-BODY TECHNIQUES

Meditation

The value of meditation is under debate by many. Some athletes swear by it and other laugh at it. Meditation is almost a form of imagery. The body is relaxed through meditation. Meditation does not bring into the mind thoughts of hockey. Meditation is basically a relaxation control of the body and mind. Meditation is also claimed to improve concentration as it disciplines the mind. It also relaxes the muscles and nerves. Anxiety, frustrations, emotions and other mental factors can be lessened by meditating. The lessening of these factors often free the body and spirit for better performance. Good performance is often the result of a clear and relaxed mind. The clear mind has no confused thoughts. The clear mind is able to send clear and precise signals to the muscles. The precise signals tell the muscles how to react correctly for proper skill execution.

Autogenic Training

Autogenic training is similar to imagery, meditation, and auto hypnosis or self-hypnosis. The European and Soviet athletes are usually well trained in this form of mental conditioning. The training consists of producing warmth and heaviness in the body.

1. In stages, the various body parts are put into deep relaxation. For example "the right arm is getting heavier and heavier. It is getting extremely heavy. It will not lift up." When the body is completely relaxed and heavy through this technique, the second stage begins.

2. The technique used to put the body in a heavy state is repeated to put the body in a warm state.

3. The same technique is used to control the heartbeat and calm the body. The self-talk is "my heartbeat is getting slower and my body is getting calmer".

4. This stage works on controlled breathing. The self-talk is "my breathing is slow and easy." If necessary, force yourself to breathe slow and easy.

5. Focus on the solar plexus and make it warm.

6. Focus on the forehead and make it cool.

An autogenic training session should last about 15 to 30 minutes. Results are not overnight. Two months or more are needed to reach maximum results.

Autogenic training with imagery

The second stage of autogenic training comes when the athlete has mastered the six stages of autogenic training and is able to put the body under autogenic control quickly. While under autogenic control the athlete adds imagery. The imagery can be of skill execution or abstract traits, like calmness, anxiety control, confidence and the performance of "flow." Flow is the super state of performance.

Choking

All mistakes are not choking. Many times failure to perform is simply the percentages falling into place. A hockey player not scoring on a breakaway to the goal is called for choking. Actually the percentages are not good when scoring on a breakaway. In fact, the goaltender has the advantage on such a breakaway. A coach must be extremely careful when accusing anyone of choking. Sometimes it is possible that a choking situation is not a choke but a lack of practice. The athlete failed because the coach never had him practice the situation. A player not performing well on a penalty shot may be the result of the coach failing to practice or condition the athlete for penalty shots during the practice sessions.

A true choke is usually the result of anxiety or pressure on the athlete. The mind is usually focusing on the outcome rather than on the execution of the skill. An athlete may muff the penalty shot because he is more worried about what will happen if he fails to score, or what will the coach do to him, or how his teammates will react, or what will the fans think. The mind has forgotten how to go about the shot as the mind is in a state of worry and confusion.

A chronic choker can be helped with the mental strategies outlined in this book. It is important to also work on the physical skill execution with the mental practice. Improvement in physical skill gives an athlete true confidence in his ability.

6

ZEN AND HOCKEY

Zen is simplicity. It is a means of achieving self control through simple procedures. Learning self control is not so difficult, but it is time consuming and requires practice, lots of practice. To learn Zen one must practice Zen. If you are learning to concentrate — practice concentration. In time you will be able to concentrate unconsciously. There will be no wrinkled brow and squinting eyes. There is no tension of the muscles. Unconscious concentration is easy, relaxed and not forced. It happens.

CONCENTRATION

If you want to concentrate on something, don't concentrate on it. If you want to concentrate on something just focus on it, freely and easily. Don't make a big deal about it. Don't force your concentration. Let the mind clear and go into "emptiness" or "nothingness." Concentration must be experienced and practiced. Concentration is not taught or read, it is learned by doing it.

Relaxation and concentration go together. They are one. Try too hard to do something and you probably fail. Forced concentration ties up the body. Concentration is an effortless effort. It is a lack of concern on the outcome. A concern for the outcome distracts the moment. Remember, a concern for the outcome is thinking of the future — a no-no. Concentration is the moment. Relax the body and mind. Let the unconscious perform.

HERE AND NOW

Everything is here and now. The mind must focus on the here and now. Actions must be geared to the here and now, the moment. A hockey game is played for the moment. The next shift will take care of itself. The moment is played as if it is the last moment of life. No carelessness, no easing up. The mind is clear of the past and free of the future. It is the here and now, the moment that takes all of the player's energy and ability. There is no let up. This playing to the moment must be practiced. It does not come with hope or wishful thinking. It comes with practice, lots of practice.

NEVER SHOW DEFEAT OR WEAKNESS.

No matter how bad things are going, a player should act as if everything is under control. He should carry on as if he are winning. Never let the opposition think they have the victory. If a team hangs their heads in defeatism, the opposition rallies in confidence. The pressure is off the opposition so they relax their worries. The opposition is now confident and relaxed. While a team is in a defeatist state, the opposition becomes dangerous and efficient.

By never showing defeat, the opposition must worry about the level of confidence. How can a losing team be so confident? They must not be defeated as of yet. Also, by acting as if winning, the winning attitude will carry over into performance. Phenomenal results have been achieved by not giving up. Come backs are not accomplished by negative thoughts. Remember to play for the moment. If a player acts defeated because of the score, then he is playing in the past and you have let yourself determine the future. There is no score for the moment. Take advantage of it.

HIGH SPIRIT/LOW SPIRIT

When performing, a player should never let his spirit deviate from normal. Too high a spirit may bring tension and loss of focus. This is what happens when the athlete celebrates before it is over. It happens in the dying minutes or seconds of the game when the team goes into a shell with careless execution to protect their lead. Too low a spirit and the body becomes careless and gives up. When the challenge presents itself, the hockey player remains normal, calm and not reckless. The player must remain spirited, but not over-spirited or under-spirited. This is control and it must be practiced.

FEAR

Fear is the first enemy. Fear is what a person makes it. Past experiences and thought processes give us our fear. An individual's perception of the situation creates fear. In athletics, fear is a constant companion. Fear is a battle with the self. All athletes know and experience fear. There is no reason for fear. Think about it. What is there to be afraid of? Fear is like a shadow — it is there but it has no substance. Often fear is caused by the uncertainty of the situation and a person's inability to cope with the situation. The situation is a threat to the ego — a person may look bad — he may fail. The fear of failure prevents a player from letting himself go. Let go of the ego and the ego cannot be under attack. Free the mind and take control. Become the situation. Be the situation. Be one.

TENSION

Tension, both mental and physical, deteriorates skill execution. When playing a player must be able to recognize when tension is creeping into his muscles. Extreme tension is readily noticeable but subtle tension is often undetected or ignored. Learning to recognize tension can be practiced very easily. When away from the ice rink, the players should tense the muscle and feel the tension of the muscle and then relax the muscle and feel the relaxation. If the players practice this several times, they soon will be able to recognize a tense muscle and a relaxed muscle. Players should practice this tension and relaxation to various parts of the body, like the arms, the legs, the forearms, etc. As the team acquires the feel for tension and relaxation, they should adapt the same procedure during a game. By recognizing tension during a game, an athlete can relax his body. Soon the hockey player will be able to better control his body and mind.

PATIENCE

Good players know patience. Patience is not being slow and lazy. Patience is when a player moves his own pace, his own internal clock. The good athlete plays to the moment and does not worry about time running out. The hockey player does not panic and worry about the situation. Panic and worry is playing to the future and not to the moment.

AWARENESS

Hockey is a game of awareness, and it must be played in a complete awareness state. Awareness does not mean knowledge of everything that is going on around the player. It does not mean knowing what all of the opponents are doing. Awareness is the awareness of an individual in his surroundings. It is a oneness. The player and the surrounding are one. The player is the game. The player is the puck. The puck is the player. It is all one. Awareness is an experience. It must be experienced, and it must be practiced.

Hockey players must develop this awareness, as it helps in the passing and shooting skills, the positional play, and the movement of both teams. The aware player reacts to the situation, it is automatic. The player "flows." Flow is the super state that some athletes have experienced at one time. It is the state of super human performance. Athletes who describe this state claim that it is as if time stood still or moved in slow motion. No matter how fast the game is played the player in the state of flow feels he has so much time to react. There is no rushing of the play. It flows smoothly and efficiently.

In hockey, a player learns mastery of the self. A mastery that carries over into everyday life. The player is in awareness with the rink, the opposition, the referees, etc. When a player can achieve this, the player is in the state of flow. The magic state when everything just flows in perfect harmony.

The mind creates the state of flow. If the mind is upset or frustrated the state of flow cannot be achieved. When the mind is upset, the body is dysfunctional. When the mind is calm, the body can respond to action, quickly and accurately. When a player move unconsciously it is as if the body thinks. The muscles react through muscle memory. The player sees — he reacts. No need to think. Hockey is such a fast paced game, the athlete must react. There is no time to think. Learning how to react comes about through practice and experience.

Practice of physical skills is essential to capture muscle memory. The physical skill is essential so that the mind can learn to trust the body. If the physical skill is not practiced and executed successfully then the mind has difficulty trusting the body. The mind cannot be deceived into thinking the body can execute something it has not done in the past or is not capable of doing. Develop the skill and the mind will trust the body.

ENLIGHTENMENT

Talent, equipment, and technology have been tremendous factors in the improvement of hockey and life. However, the use of one's talent, equipment and technology is still dependent on the mind. The mind controls all the factors. The mind decides how to use these factors to advantage. The ability to win or succeed is, and will continue to be, decided by the mind. The use of the mind determines one's final success. Better warriors think better. Better warriors have better mind control. The best warrior has the best mind control of all the warriors. Hockey players are warriors.

Mind control is the key to hockey enlightenment. The great Japanese swordsman Munenori claimed that he used swordsmanship to learn how to control the mind. As his mind control developed, his swordsmanship was able to perform through the Will. Hockey is the same way. Use hockey to learn to control the mind and then let hockey be performed by the Will. Performing by the Will is the enlightened stage.

The mind controls the body. It is the mind that moves the arms and legs. When we use the Will we are using our intuition. It is important to know that the mind is not the brain. The mind is the mind. The brain is the physical organ in the head. The mind is in the muscles, bones, skin, etc. The mind is in the body, the whole body. With the mind in the body, the body is able to react quickly without thought. Thinking takes time. Thought impulses must travel from the brain to the muscles of the body. This is too slow for quick movements of hockey. The brain is inactive and empty. The mind is ready, always ready, if the mind is aware and alert. To reach the stage of enlightenment one must let the mind move from the brain and into the body — the entire body.

To reach the stage of enlightenment you must master all things you do. When you have not mastered a skill, you will have doubts about how to do the skill. Your mind has doubts. Since the mind controls the body, the doubting mind transfers the doubts to confuse the body. Develop your skills to eliminate confusion in the mind. When you perform, be clear in your mind.

It is a disease to be obsessed with the thought of winning.

It is a disease to be obsessed with the thought of failure.

It is a disease to be obsessed with the thought of anything.

Obsession sickens the mind. The obsessed mind is clouded. The enlightened mind is alert and aware of all factors. Obsession on a factor does not develop the full picture. The warrior's obsessed mind is on a single factor and not the big picture. The obsessed mind has become attached. The mind must never become attached. This is not the way of the warrior. The attached mind is a stuck mind, a slow mind, a diseased mind. The enlightened athlete must not let his mind become obsessed.

When enlightened, a player sees with his mind. When the mind sees it, the eyes notice it. The mind controls the body, even the eyes. The arms and legs see with the mind. The arms and legs perform their skills through their own eyesight. This is the ultimate stage of learning — the intuition stage. The intuition stage is much like a reflex. The skill is performed automatically with no conscious thought.

To be a hockey warrior, the player must practice all the principles in this book. Reading alone will not do it. Reading and practice must go together. Without practice, the player cannot find the Way. The Way is the way of the Hockey Warrior.

Section 3

Coaching Duties and Organization

The coach must be an organized man. The following chapters will help the coach plan and organize the program. Team harmony and player attitudes can be strongly affected through management.

7

THE PLAYERS' EQUIPMENT

Hockey equipment can be expensive; however, it is essential and vital to the protection of the player. The coach must have a thorough knowledge of what is needed and the purpose of each piece of equipment for the calibre of play in question. This knowledge will help the coach to select good equipment in the proper price range.

In selecting the equipment, the coach should always remember that an injury due to cheap equipment is not money saved. The best possible protection should be mandatory. A good rule to follow is to spend more on the protective equipment and save the expense on the coverings like the sweaters and socks.

If it is possible, the coach should order equipment from personally inspected samples. Such considerations as stitching, design, fit and workmanship are readily noticeable. Material should also be checked for shrinkage, color fastness and color luster. Actual samples will give the coach a good understanding of an item much better than a picture in a catalogue.

Time and money can be saved by ordering stock items. Special or custom designs are usually more expensive. If ordering a special design be sure to provide a clear, accurate and detailed description of the item. Such a description can save a heartache later on if the manufacturer makes a mistake on the order.

Equipment should be stored in a dry, well ventilated area. Keep the storage area organized and neat. It can be a real hassle when one has to look all over for some items. All equipment should be repaired and cleaned before it is stored. This makes the equipment ready for the next season. Equipment delayed in repairing will often result in a major expense instead of a minor expense. If the delay is too long the item may not be worth the repair.

Dressing rooms should be arranged and designed so that equipment can be hung up after each game and practice. This procedure gives the equipment a chance to properly dry. The coach must enforce a tidy dressing room with all equipment properly hung up.

SKATES

Most often, the better known brands are the best choice. Good skate companies have considerable experience in skate building and designing and are able to make the best skate for the money.

In selecting skates, the fit and construction are most important. The boot should feel snug and yet comfortable. The width of the boot is very important and yet often ignored as most people think in terms of length only. It is usually best to wear a thin pair of socks with the skates. Thin socks keep the skates snug to the feet. Some players wear no socks for a better feel.

Some players prefer to wear custom made skates for an exact fit. Most players will find the regular line models more than adequate in fit and price. The regular lines are less expensive and readily available. If a player is used to the regular lines, a broken skate can be readily replaced on a short notice. Custom skates usually take time to be made and shipped.

Many factors are involved in deciding upon the pricing and quality of skates. The financial status of the player, the budget of the team, and the calibre of play are some of the factors in determining what to pay for skates. Fortunately, good skates can be purchased without having to buy the top line model.

A good skate should have a strong and well constructed heel and ankle support. Cheap skates are very weak in this area. This is usually not a problem with the plastic boot, but it should be checked. Better quality skates have a higher pitch. The pitch is the relationship of the heel to the toes with the heel higher than the toes. The better skates also have better and harder steel in the skate blade. The harder steel will hold their edge better and longer after sharpening.

If the skates are properly constructed, ankle supports should not be needed. Weak ankles is a term used to explain ankles that are turned in or out while trying to skate. Actually, the term is a misnomer for a lack of balance. Usually the skater's ankles are not "weak" as they serve quite well in other sports or skills. This balance problem can often be the result of poorly constructed skates or poor fitting skates.

Breaking in a pair of skates is usually an unwelcome duty. Leather skates are often more difficult but the process can be speeded up by wearing the skates with wet socks. Some players simply soak the new skates in water, lace them up and wear them for practice. With plastic skates, the fit of the skate at purchase is vital as the plastic skate will not mold to the foot as the leather does.

A hockey player must take very good care of his skates. The blades should be wiped clean and dry after each use. If the blade is allowed to rust, the rusting action eats at the steel and can result in a poor edge when sharpened. Care should be taken when walking in skates to prevent nicks and dullness to the blade. Entrances to the ice and dressing room should be kept clean and free of anything that can dull or damage the skate blade edge. The skate blade edge is the only thing that gives the player contact with the ice, so it must be sharpened expertly and treated with great care when off the ice.

HOCKEY STICKS

Hockey sticks are usually a major expense. The coach should be familiar with the different companies and their price ranges. He should order a good stick that will serve the players and the budget. A hockey stick becomes a very personal item to a player. He trusts his stick. A poor quality stick that does not meet the demands of the team can give the players a loss of confidence and a low team moral. Some companies will even put the team name on the hockey stick and color the stick to the team's colors. Goal sticks are also expensive. Some goal sticks hold up better than others, so care should be taken when ordering such sticks.

SUPPORTER AND PROTECTIVE CUP

These items are required and easily purchased. Goalies should have their own style of large protection. Most of these items are very similar. It is usually a question of what equipment will hold up the best over time.

GARTER BELT

Like the supporters, poor quality garter belts will easily tear and wear and become unserviceable. It is often worth a few extra dollars for a better constructed garter belt.

PROTECTIVE PADDING

The coach should order good quality shin pads that provide excellent protection to the front of the shins and knees and to the side of the leg. The protective padding should not be bulky or cumbersome. The length of the pad is important for proper fitting on the leg of the player.

Elbow pads are important to the player. Some pads are too bulky and awkward. The size of the pad will depend on the size of the player.

Like the elbow pads, the size and expense of the shoulder pads will vary according to the age, size, and ability of the players. Usually the forward's style is smaller and lighter than the defensemen's pads with the extra chest and arm protection.

CHEST PROTECTORS

This is a goaltender's item. The protector must be a good fit and not cumbersome to the wearer. In addition to these qualities, it must offer excellent protection as the goaltender will be tested with many shots to the chest area. If the protector does not provide maximum protection the goaltender may develop a fear of shots to the chest. This is one item where the best is needed.

HOCKEY PANTS

Hockey pants are designed to protect the vulnerable areas of kidneys, coccyx (tail bone), hips and thighs. Pants should be checked to be sure that they provide the best protection possible. Try not to order pants that are too big for the players. If the pants are too large for the player the protective padding shifts around the player and may not be in the correct position when contact is made. A thigh pad that does not hug the thigh may shift off the thigh during a body check and leave the player with a severe injury. Pants with the tapered leg usually better hold the thigh pad in place. Hockey pants that do not fit snugly and yet comfortably may be risky to wear. Some companies now have the player's protective pads in the form of underwear so that the protective pads are held close to body and in place. The hockey pant that corresponds to this type of underwear is the shell. The hockey pant shell with the underwear type pads is the best style of pant protection to purchase.

HOCKEY GLOVES

The main emphasis in purchasing hockey gloves is the dexterity and manipulative factors along with protection. Not only do the hands need maximum protection but the protection must not hinder the agility of the hands. Good gloves usually meet these requirements; however, the gloves should be checked thoroughly. The palms of the glove are often the deciding factor on feel of the glove. Hockey gloves take a beating so be sure they are well constructed.

The goaltender's blocker and catching glove also become very personal items to the goaltender. Very often it is best to let the goaltender pick out the model that will fit and feel best to him. Also, be aware when ordering to stipulate the need of the left handed or right handed combinations.

HELMETS

Helmets are an essential piece of equipment. The fit should be snug. A loose helmet will slide around on contact or even slip off and leave the head vulnerable on contact. Protection cannot be provided with a helmet that will not stay in place to protect the area it is designed to protect. In selecting the helmet, pick a helmet with a chin strap that is easy to tighten, loosen, snap and unsnap. It is very annoying to a player when he has trouble with his chin strap.

GOAL MASKS

The mask is a very personal item. The goaltender must have a mask that is a perfect fit. He must have confidence in his mask. A mask that does not fit well is not only a nuisance, but it may also be dangerous. It is usually best to let the goaltender pick his mask.

GOAL LEG PADS

In most cases, the top line or close to the top line goal pad is best for protection and upkeep. Good goal pads hold up to the demands of play. They maintain their shape longer and last longer before wearing out. Minor repairs may regularly be needed, but this is normal. Make minor repairs immediately before the damage turns into a major repair.

MOUTHGUARDS

Mouthguards are an inexpensive item and certainly are much cheaper than dental bills. Some mouthguards can be fitted by a dentist while others can be molded to the teeth by the individual himself. Some models are boiled in water and then the player bites into the mouthguard for a molded fit.

EQUIPMENT BAGS

Equipment bags are made of various materials like canvas and vinyl. Usually the canvas style is best as there is a little breathing quality to the canvas. Vinyl does not breath and moisture inside the bag usually stays inside the bag. Hockey equipment is often packed slightly damp or even wet, so a little breathing quality can be helpful. Probably the most important feature in ordering bags is to be sure the size is large enough and that the goaltenders get the larger goaltender model. Be sure the stitching is strong. Check the carrying straps to be sure the straps are securely fastened to the bag. The straps should be designed so that the weight of the bag is evenly distributed through the straps. The suitcase style is easier to carry, pack and handle than the other styles like the duffle bag.

8

COACHING DUTIES

Coaching is a year-round job. The off-season should be used to formulate plans and organize for the coming season. Beginning the season in an orderly manner will enhance a smooth progression from the off-season to the preseason to the season. Good organization will give the players a feeling of confidence with the coach and management. Disruptions will occur, but the well-prepared coach will be ready to meet these disruptions. A coach should always plan for "Murphy's Law," whatever can go wrong will go wrong. A coach that plans for these problems will be prepared for them if they do occur.

PRESEASON ARRANGEMENTS

Arrangements for facilities, equipment and training should be made before the season starts. Many of these things will be done during the off-season. If they are done during the off-season then they should be checked and verified during the preseason so that all systems are go when the season actually starts.

PRACTICE PLANNING

Practice planning is a combination of long range goals and short term goals. The coach must develop his long range goals from his philosophy of the game. His desired style of play for the future years are part of the long range goal. His short term goals are a lead-up to his long range plans and his philosophy.

This planning takes time and should not be treated lightly. Plan so you know where you are going and how you are going to get there.

We practice our skills over and over until we have improved or mastered them. Repetition, at least correct repetition, is a key factor in learning and retaining our skills. Learning skills requires time, lots of time. The coach must give adequate time to learning, retaining and refining the skills of the game. The coaches practice planning must reflect this time requirement.

Drills and practice planning should be designed from game conditions. Drills should reflect game conditions. The way the coach wants it played during a game is the way it should be practiced. If the game plan is for short passes then the practice should be planned around the short passing game.

To save ice time, the coach should do his talking and explaining in the dressing room before going on the ice. A chalk board or any other type of visual aid can be used to explain the practice and the drills to the players. This means ice time is saved by not having to explain things on the ice. Long discussions on the ice is dead time. Sometimes on-ice discussions are needed, but, if ice time is expensive and you are only allowed so much time or budget, keep the on-ice practice moving and do the long talks in the dressing room.

In most cases, the coach should have his players demonstrate skills in practice. This gives recognition to the player and helps with the player's confidence. With the players demonstrating, the coach is free to comment on technique and point out the key points in the skill. As a coach gets older, his demonstrations may not be as good as he thinks they are. Some coaches' demonstrations seem to be a means of "showing off" or showing how good they are. Be careful, do not let this happen to you. Some coaches demonstrate because they do not know how to adequately comment on the technique. They know how to do the skill, but they do not know how to teach the skill. Another important consideration in demonstrations is that when one demonstrates, the observers or players will focus on the results of the demonstration and not on the technique of the skill. For example, if the coach is demonstrating slap shot accuracy, the players will focus on how accurate his shot is and not on the technique.

Practice sessions need variety and interest and the coach should not let the practices become routine or stereotypical. Usually there are many drills that can accomplish the same purpose so it is advisable to vary the drills to help maintain interest. With this in mind, the coach should be careful to not use a drill so much that it becomes routine. Boredom and carelessness may set in.

It is a good idea for the coach to keep his practice plans with him for rechecking and evaluation. If a coach finds that his breakout play is not working, he can check his plans for time allotment on the breakout play. If the check reveals that insufficient time was spent on the breakout then future practices can be adjusted accordingly. If sufficient time was given to the breakout play, the coach must decide why it is not working. Perhaps the learning situation was not good, maybe the coaching was inadequate, maybe the style of teaching is not working with this group, or maybe the players are slow learners. These are difficult questions to answer honestly. It is not easy to say the coaching was weak despite all the work and effort that went into the practices. Work and effort at times are not enough as it is results that count. Evaluate honestly and correct your errors.

The practice plans should remain flexible. If some phases are not progressing as fast as predicted then future sessions have to be adjusted to meet this demand. The plan for the day, however, should usually remain the same. Adjustments are for the next day. Too many last minute adjustment during the day plan will throw off the overall plan. If a 15 minute period is allowed for penalty killing, and success is not achieved in the period, then move on to the next drill and adjust the plan for tomorrow and other succeeding practice sessions. By doing this procedure, the coach has time to analyze the situation for corrective measures.

The coach should outline what he wants to develop for the season. This season plan is then broken down into smaller units, perhaps into weekly or bimonthly units. The units are then broken down into the individual practice sessions.

SAMPLE PRACTICE PLAN

Plan for the week: Puck control emphasis.

Monday: 2 hours	Thursday: 2 hours
Tuesday: 2 hours	Friday: 2 hours
Wednesday: 2 hours	Saturday: 2 hours

Total 12 hours = 720 minutes

Breakdown for the week: 12 hours = 720 minutes

GAMEPHASE	TIME(minutes)	SKILL	TIME (minutes)
Skating	100	Forward	20
		Backward	40
		Lateral	40
Puck control	300	Stickhandling	100
		Passing and	
		Pass receiving	100
		shooting	100

Offense	120	Basic attack	60
		Breakout	60
Defense	120	Forechecking	60
		Stickchecking	30
		Backchecking	30
Situations	60	One on one	15
		Two on one	15
		Two on two	15
		Three on two	15

Total time allotted for the week: 720 minutes

Total time planned for the week: 700

Time left over for cushion: 20

Daily practice: MONDAY

TIME   DRILL

2:40	Meeting, orientation for practice. Be dressed at this time.
2:50	Free time on ice.
3:00	**Skating** (10 minutes)

Forward

Breaking between blue lines - 4 min.

Backward

Figure 8 - 4 min.

Lateral

Mirror drill - 2 min.

3:10   **Puck control** (50 minutes)

Stickhandling

Laps - 5 min.

Passing

Stationary 20 feet apart - 5 min.

Stationary backhand - 5 min.

Give and take - 15 min.

Shooting

Slap shot inside blue line - 10 min.

Deking and fake shot - 10 min.

4:00   **Offense** (20 minutes)

Drop pass on blue line - 4 min.

Back pass to blue line - 4 min.

Back pass to partner and shoot - 12 min.

4:20   **Defense** (20 minutes)

Forechecking in corner - 10 min.

Stickchecking partners - 10 min.

4:40   **Situations** (10 minutes)

One on one - 5 min.

Two on one - 5 min.

4:50   **Skating** (8 minutes)
          Stop and start on whistle - 2 min.
          Length of ice - 2 min.
          Backward agility - 2 min.
          Scooting - 2 min.

4:58   **Cool down**

SAMPLE CHECK LIST

The check list is an excellent means of recording how much time is spent on each phase of the game. All possible skills or situations are listed down the side of a sheet of paper. Under the date column the time in minutes is recorded. As the season progresses the coach can evaluate his time allotments.

SKILL	DATE: NOVEMBER						
	1	2	3	4	5	6	7
Conditioning	10	5	10	15			
Skating	15	15	10	15			
Stickhandling	10	15	5	15			
Passing	20	15	20	10			
Shooting	10	15	10	15			
Checking	5	15	5	15			
Individual skills							
defensemen	10	10	10				
forwards	10	10	10				
Offensive play	20	20	15				
Defensive play							
Face-offs			5	5			
Penalty killing							
Power play							
Pulled goalie	15						
Line changes	10						
Delayed penalty							
Broken stick	5						
Injuries							
TOTAL	120	120	115	90			

DISCIPLINE

A hockey technique should never be used as a disciplinary measure. Many coaches use extra skating or stop-and-start drill as a form of punishment. This form of punishment uses a desired result like hard skating in a negative situation. Hard skating is what a coach needs in his players and so hard skating should be a reward and not a punishment. Extra laps given in fun or for conditioning are not only beneficial but can help to boost team morale. Discipline problems are usually best handled off the ice.

IMPORTANCE OF UNDERSTANDING THE ATHLETE

The coach should gain as much knowledge of his players as possible. He is working with human beings and not robots. A knowledge of his player's backgrounds, attitudes, and desires will help the coach understand his players. Getting to know and helping the players is a year-round job.

As players move up in age and league status, the competition becomes keener and tougher. The better players remain, and the poorer player drop out. First year players who have just moved up to a higher calibre of play must adjust to not only the higher level of play but also to the different social level of the team. Some player can handle the playing level but have problems with the new team environment and different players. Some players were stars at the lower level and now must cope with the situation of being a regular or even a below average player in the higher league. This can be a tremendous psychological strain on the player. Such players may lose confidence and may even desire to quit the team. The coach must be aware of these types of problems and make every effort to prevent the collapse of a player. Patience, understanding and guidance can help some players. Coaches must recognize potential or possible potential and help the player. The coach will not always be successful but it is worth a try.

PERSONAL CONTACT

The importance of personal contact with the players must be fully realized by the coach. The coach should always be with his team whenever the team is together as a unit. If he is absent, the players may feel the coach has let them down or the occasion is not that important. During game situations, the coach should be in the dressing room to meet the arrival of the players. By being the first on the scene the coach may be able to set the tone and atmosphere before the game. The coach should also be with the team between periods to set the tone and control the environment for the next period. After the players have settled down, the coach will be able to discuss plans and answer questions.

COACHING UNIFORM

Dress properly. Always be warm. Nothing can be more annoying than being slightly cold during practice or a game. Usually, it is best to have some kind of uniform for practice. A sweat suit is most common and serves quite well. Some may like a jacket and pants. Some like a sweater instead of a jacket. If the coach is wearing a special uniform, the players feel that he is serious about his job and means business.

MANAGERS

The selection of a manager is extremely important. He is a key person and is as valuable as any player. The manager is valuable for team moral. A good, happy manager can help instill the same attitude with the team. A manager is a link between the player and the coach and his understanding of the players can be an asset to the coach. The manager must be loyal, trustworthy and dependable. If he cannot meet these demands than dismissal may be appropriate. The manager must be available when the players need him. Often the manager may be required for minor injuries and first-aid unless a team trainer is with the team. If the team has more than one manager, then each manager must have his duties defined so that there is no overlap of functions or confusion of tasks. Good managers often go unnoticed despite the fact that the smooth operation of the team may depend on them. A wise coach will make his manager well aware of his contribution to the team.

TEAM CAPTAINS

The team captain or captains are appointed or elected. The choice is up to the coach. The captain is the liaison between the players and the coach. The responsibility given to the captain is dependent on the coach. Some captains are given duties and responsibilities while some are only figure heads. There are advantages and disadvantages as to whether the captains are elected or appointed, with duties or no duties. The coach must evaluate his situation.

LEGAL LIABILITY

A coach must always be aware of legal liability. If uninsured, he may want to protect himself with insurance. The following rules may be helpful.

1. Never leave your players unsupervised.

2. Know first-aid, but do not overstep into the duties of a doctor.

3. Do not let a player run the risk of injury through your negligence. The safety and care of the players is the coach's responsibility.

4. Try to have a doctor at all home games and practices.

5. Never give pep pills or any type of drugs to the players. Leave this to the doctor.

6. Do not allow anyone to participate without a medical examination or parental approval in the lower leagues.

7. Make all recommendations for safety measures in writing to your superiors. Keep one copy and the other to the league, school, owner, or whoever is responsible.

8. Insist on hygiene and safety at all times.

Recommendations for hygiene would be safe showers, clean equipment, clean dressing rooms, etc. Each player must hang up his own equipment and put waste, tape, etc. in the refuse can. There should be no throwing of tape, snow from the skates, or anything that may be dangerous to the eyes.

ACADEMIC STANDING

Good grades are important for school teams. Most teams and leagues have rules on academic qualification. If necessary, study halls may be needed. Some schools have a tutor system to help the athletes. Some colleges are now hiring Academic Counselors to keep the athletes eligible. A coach must continually monitor his player's grades so that he is aware of each player's standing.

TRAVELING DRESS AND BEHAVIOR

Players should dress up for travel. The attire will depend on the age group and type of travel. Youngsters need not by required to wear special clothes but their clothes should be clean and neat. Economic problems may have a bearing on the quality of clothes, but it should not prevent the rule of cleanliness and neatness. The coach should insist on orderly and mannerly behavior at all times. In some cases, especially in the younger leagues, the coach may have to teach such things as manners, respect and appropriate behavior.

SLUMPS OR STALENESS

Staleness results when no learning takes place. The coach should always try to keep a learning situation in the daily practices. Sometimes the slumps come even though preventative measures are taken. Usually, if an athlete is giving an all-out effort all the time, he is susceptible to a slump. If an athlete never has a slump then he may be suspect of not giving his all. Staleness may be suffered by an individual or the team. Various tactics may be successful to bring a player out of a slump. Which one will work is never known until it is tried. Some of the tactics are to check a player's technique. A change in routine may help. An increase in the work load has proven helpful. Short practice sessions and canceled practices often help.

DIET

In most cases, the coach will have no control over the diet of his players. Such control lies with the parents or the player's themselves. Although the coach may not have control of diet, he should make sure that his players are aware of how to achieve good nutrition for health and energy.

SLEEP AND REST

An athlete should keep fairly regular sleeping hours. Proper rest through the week will counter any sleep loss on game night. Care should be taken in not getting too much sleep. Too much sleep causes dullness. Eight to nine hours a night is sufficient to restore the body to peak efficiency. More than this may well decondition the body.

On game day, the importance of rest is often overemphasized. The sluggishness and dullness caused by too much sleep affects the athlete both physically and mentally. Physically, the athlete is slow and heavy. Mentally, the athlete is not alert. A little exercise or a work out on game day is often advantageous to the athlete in preparing him for the game.

SELECTING THE TEAM

One of the most difficult parts of coaching is the selection of players for the team. Every player must be given a fair chance to display his talents. If a player is cut, he should be able to talk to the coach to find out why he did not make the team or to explain why his performance was not up to par. Sometimes it is advisable to give the player another chance to prove himself. When the player has another chance he often gets a closer look for evaluation. Giving players a retry not only sets up a procedure of fairness, but it is especially fair when ice time is scarce and the tryout procedure is shorter than usual. At the beginning of the season, some players take time to adjust and get ready for the team. The coach must not be too quick to cut.

As an aid to selection, the coach may find a rating system helpful. A rating system forces the coach to look at all the important features of a player. Often when the coach relies on just observation without notation it is possible to miss an important aspect of a player. A rating system can help the coach in organizing this difficult task. There may be nothing worse than cutting a player through a poor and inefficient evaluation system.

Figure 1 is a sample chart of a rating system. A coach may devise a system to meet his needs. Each skill is rated on a scale of 1 to 5 with 1 as the top score. The overall rating is the total score with the lowest score being the best score. It is possible that some players may score poorly in the overall total but have some outstanding features or scores on some skills. These outstanding individual skill scores may give the coach reason for keeping or for more look over. However these scores are used, the scores should not be the final criteria. The scores are only an aid to evaluation and selection.

NAME	NO	SKATING	SHOOTING	PASSING	PASS RECEIVING	STICK HANDLING	HOCKEY SENSE	POTENTIAL	RATING	COMMENTS
WALLS	2	1	2	2	3	3	2	1	14	GOOD PROSPECT
JONES	3	5	2	4	5	4	5	4	32	NO CHANCE
DUNN	4	2	3	3	3	2	2	1	16	PROMISE

Figure 8-1: A Rating System for Team Selection

TESTING

In selecting a team, the coach may find that testing the players in certain game skills can be very helpful. As in the rating system, the testing program is a guide and not the final criteria. Tests can help give the coach a look at potential of some players. Players with excellent skill scores but have low scores in game-like condition drills may have mental problems in adjusting to game conditions.

The following is a hockey skill test devised by the author for a M.S. degree requirement. The validity and reliability of this test is very high.

Overall Procedures:

1. All times are stopped when the first skate touches the finish line.

2. All times should be recorded to the nearest tenth of a second.

3. A performer is allowed two tries for each event with the best score counting.

4. All starts are from a motionless standing start.

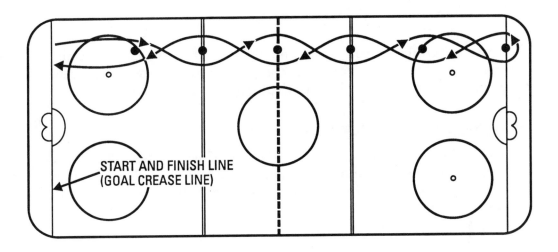

Figure 8-2: Puck Carry Test

PUCK CARRY TEST

The puck is placed on the goal crease line and the player stands behind the crease line with his skates facing straight ahead and the feet side by side. The player must carry the puck weaving around each obstacle to the end and back. If the player loses the puck, his time continues as he recovers and resumes progress at the point of error. If two or more obstacles are knocked over the score is disqualified and the run counts as an attempt.

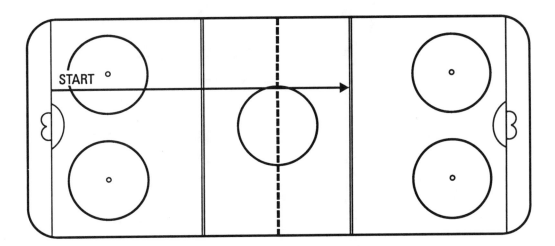

Figure 8-3: Speed Forward and Backward Test

SPEED FORWARD TEST

The player starts behind the crease line with his feet side by side and facing straight ahead. The player skates as fast as possible to the second blue line. If the player falls, his time continues until he crosses the finish line.

SPEED BACKWARD TEST

The speed backward test is the same as the speed forward test. The player starts from a motionless stand with his back to the finish line. The performer is not allowed to pivot to forward skating and back to backward skating in order to build up speed.

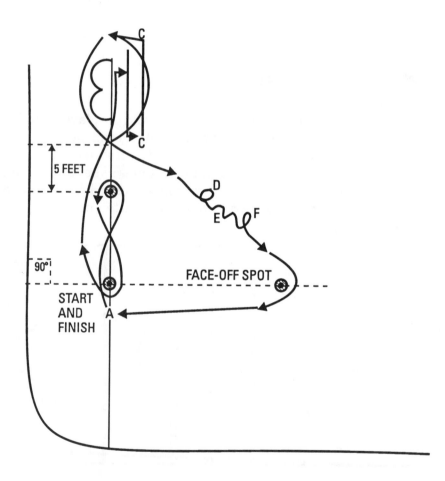

Figure 8-4: Agility Test

AGILITY TEST

The performer starts by straddling the goal crease line at 'A'. The hockey stick must be held below waist level at all times during the run. At 'C' the performer must cross the goal crease line with both feet, stop and go. At 'D' the player pivots to backward skating and then must take at least one backward stride at 'E' and then return to forward skating at 'F'.

SHOOTING TESTS

The shooting test does not have the high validity as the other four tests. Despite this fact they can be used for a "look see" and interest factor. The players enjoy doing these tests to see how they compare with each other.

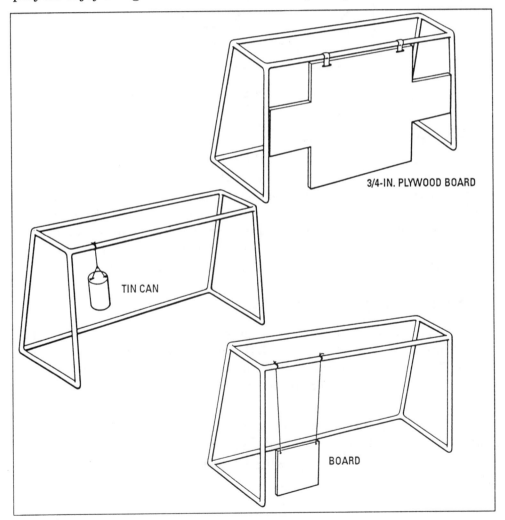

Figure 8-5: Shooting Targets

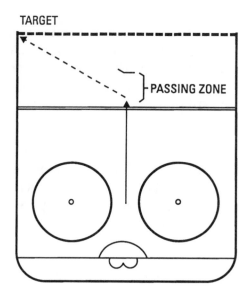

Figure 8-6: Passing Test

PASSING TEST

The passing test is not as valid as the other tests but it does give some indication as to skill. A hockey stick is placed on the ice halfway between the red line and the blue line. The player skates toward the hockey stick and is required to make the pass between the stick and the blue line while skating and not stopping. In most cases the blue line on the boards can be used as the target. If this is too small a target then just make a larger one. The pass must be made with the puck sliding along the ice and not above the ice.

TESTING LAYOUT

The coach can administer each test himself or he can set up a rotational system where all tests are done together with the players rotating from station to station. The rotational system requires more help but it does get the testing done quicker. Some coaches prefer to administer one test at each practice as a fun time session.

Another advantage of the testing program is for youth hockey programs. Some city youth programs have used the scores to select their teams. The scores are ranked in order and then going down the list the players are assigned to teams.

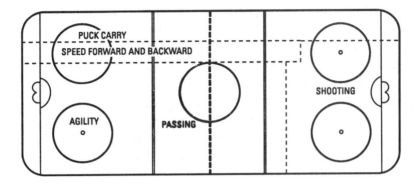

Figure 8-7: Testing Layout

PLAYER DEVELOPMENT

The coach should be concerned with the development of future players. The success of the higher level teams depends on the progression of younger talent. In most cases, the success of the high school team is a result of the quality of the youth program in the school district. The coach should always take an interest and help if possible with the youth programs. The youngsters appreciate this and will look forward to playing for such a coach.

At the university level, player development can be done with junior varsity or freshmen teams. If this is not feasible then the coach should keep some players on the team who are not quite ready for varsity level. Maybe some extra work and time is all these players need to reach their potential.

THE PREGAME WARM-UP

The following is an example of a pregame warm-up that has been used with excellent results. The warm-up covers forward and backward skating, stickhandling, puck control, passing, pass receiving, shooting, offense and defense. The goaltender receives shots from all angles as well as game condition shots.

1. Each player carries a puck onto the ice. The signal for changing drills is given by the captain yelling or whistling.
2. The players skate and stickhandle in single file in a large circle on their half of the rink.
3. The command is given, the players stop, reverse directions, skate and stickhandle in the other direction.
4. On the second command, the players join with partners and skate around in their circle giving and receiving short passes with each other.

5. On the third command, the players position themselves to one side of the ice for the two-on-one drill. As the two-on-one unit finishes their attempt, the players position themselves on the other side of the ice for the two-on-one again.

6. On the fourth command, the centermen line up in the middle ice area with their wingers to each side on the boards. A defenseman in the corner passes out to the centerman who in turn passes to a breaking winger for a shot on goal. The centerman then receives another pass from the defenseman, passes to his other winger and then goes to the back of the centermen's line. The next centerman then takes his turn at passing to his wingers.

7. On the fifth and final command, the players skate the circle backwards and follow their captain into the dressing room for the game.

BETWEEN PERIODS OF THE GAME

The coach should follow the team into the dressing room to get them settled and quiet. It is usually best to have the dressing room free of extra people. Only the coaches, players, and managers need to be in the dressing room. Extra people are distractions to the task at hand.

The managers should have cold, wet towels and dry towels to pass around. Oranges, lemons and liquid drinks should be readily available. If the coach has to talk to someone, it is best to do this outside the dressing room.

After the team has settled down, they will be more receptive to criticism or praise. By waiting until the last half of the rest period the player's minds will have cleared and tactics can be better understood. The dressing room atmosphere is important to the players. The coach should maintain this atmosphere with his leadership.

AFTER THE GAME

After the game, there is nothing that will change the outcome of the game. The game is over. Severe criticism is best saved until the next practice or next day. By waiting a day, the coach gets more time to thoroughly evaluate the game and his criticism. Also, by waiting for the next day the players have time to settle down and will be more receptive to criticism as they will have had a chance to look at themselves objectively. In many cases, the players know the criticism is coming, so the extra time gives them preparation time. Severe criticism immediately after the game usually catches the players while they are exceptionally mad, charged up and excited. It is very easy for hard feelings to occur. Rash, impulsive statements after a hard fought battle can lead to bitter resentment among the players and between the coaches and players.

9

COACHING AIDS, STATISTICS, SCOUTING AND SPOTTING

A coach should be able to present his ideas and plans in a clear, concise manner. At no time should the players be in doubt or have a misunderstanding of what is expected of them. To help in the presentation of plans, the coach may find the following aids helpful.

A calendar of events should be posted in a convenient place for all to see. Usually near the door is best, so the players can check it as they leave. The spaces should be large enough for large printing. If the coach has the time, he may be able to have posters for each game to help motivate the players.

Charts can be used as an incentive and for record keeping. Scoring charts, game rating charts, injury charts, etc., can all be helpful. An injury chart is not only a fun item with the players, but it will also provide a record of the type of injury with the players. If a certain injury seems to be fairly common then maybe there is a weakness in that segment of the conditioning program.

SUNDAY	MONDAY	TUESDAY	WEDNESDAY	THURSDAY	FRIDAY	SATURDAY
28	PRACTICE 3:00 P.M. (SWEATSUIT ONLY) 29	PRACTICE 4 P.M. 30	MEETING 2:30 PRACTICE 3:30 1	PRACTICE 4 P.M. 2	PRACTICE 3 P.M. 3	PRACTICE 10 A.M. 4
5	PRACTICE 3:00 P.M. (FULL GEAR) 6	PRACTICE 4 P.M. 7	PRACTICE 3:30 8	PRACTICE 12 NOON 2:30 PACK 9	GAME AT 8 P.M. 10	GAME AT 8 P.M. 11
12	PRACTICE 3:00 P.M. (SWEATSUITS) 13	PRACTICE 4 P.M. 14	HOME GAME WITH_____ 8 P.M. 15	PRACTICE 4 P.M. (SWEATSUITS) 16	PRACTICE 3 P.M. 17	HOME GAME WITH_____ 8 P.M. 18
HOME GAME WITH_____ 2:30 P.M. 19	NO PRACTICE 20	PRACTICE 4 P.M. 21	MEETING 2:30 PRACTICE 3:30 22	PRACTICE 4 P.M. 23	24	25

Figure 1: A Sample Calendar of Events

INJURIES	
#2 WALLS	1 - 6 STITCHES OVER EYE 2 - PULLED GROIN
#3 JONES	1 - SEPARATED SHOULDER (COLLISION IN CORNER)
#4 DUNN	1 - TORN KNEE LIGAMENTS (RIGHT KNEE) 2 - STITCHES ON CHEEK

Figure 2: A Sample Chart

GAME _____ SCORE _____ DATE _____		
PHASE	COMMENTS	RATING
PASSING	*VERY BAD - ESPECIALLY FOR BREAK OUT*	4
SHOOTING	*WEAK SHOTS - TAKING TOO LONG TO SHOOT*	3
POSITION	*FAIRLY SPOTTY - BUT COMING ALONG QUITE WELL*	2
FORECHECK	*FAIRLY GOOD - BUT STILL A LITTLE SPOTTY*	2
BACKCHECK	*FAIRLY GOOD*	2
BREAK OUT	*WEAK - POOR POSITIONAL PLAY PLUS BAD PASSING*	3
OFFENSE	*FAIRLY GOOD - STILL TAKING TOO LONG TO SWITCH TO DEFENSE*	2

Figure 3: A Sample Game Rating Chart

Figure 3 is a sample of a very simple rating chart. In the statistic section there are more detailed charts.

Chalk or Marking Boards. Dressing rooms should have a chalk or marking board. If a ready made rink is marked on the board then it becomes that much better. Some coaches have small boards to carry in their hands to use while behind the bench.

Magnetic Boards. Some chalk and marking boards are magnetized so the magnets representing the players can be moved around. Different colors for different teams. Some coaches like these, some do not. Small magnetic boards are available for use behind the bench.

Video. Video has become indispensable to some coaches. If used properly it can be a very helpful item. The expense of video equipment is continually going down so it becomes more available. If it is not in the budget, most teams have a team member or a parent who has one.

A Note Pad. This little item is valuable. It should be carried at all times to jot down those spur of the moment ideas.

Small Tape Recorder. Some coaches like to carry one during games or when scouting. Comments are put on tape and then analyzed later.

Music. Music can be an interesting aspect during skating drills. Some teams like music during the pregame preparation in the dressing room.

CHARTS

Shot Chart. Most teams record shots on goal with a shot chart. In some leagues this is mandatory. Figure 4 is a sample shot chart. A coach can devise his own chart to meet his needs although most charts are similar.

The shot chart is used for only one period. The coach can readily evaluate how his team is shooting and from where. Is the team getting any shots from the slot? The number on the chart is the player's number and the position from where the shot was taken. If a goal is scored, then a circle is drawn around the number. A number with a stroke through it is a shot that missed the goal. An unmarked number is a shot that the goalie stopped.

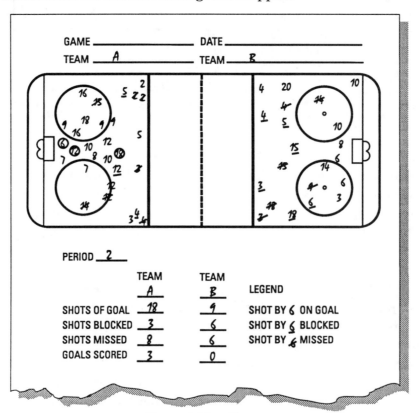

Figure 4: Shot Chart

GOALS SCORED CHART

The goals scored chart can be added to the shot chart. A record of where the goals are scored may indicate a weakness of the goaltender to this area. These charts should be kept throughout the season for future games against certain goaltenders and for checking your own goaltender. If your own goaltender shows a trend to a certain area, you will know what to work on.

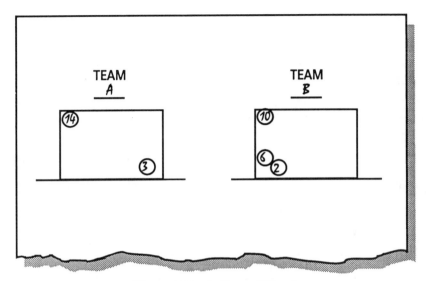

Figure 5: Goals Scored Chart

FOR/AGAINST CHART

The ice time for goals will provide a record of who was on the ice for goals scored and for goals against. The numbers represent the player's jersey number.

FACE-OFF CHART

A record of the face-offs won and lost can be helpful. If the won-lost ratio is bad then practice in this area is essential.

SAMPLE SCOUTING FORMS

The sample scouting form shown here is quite detailed. Coaches should modify this sample to meet their needs. It may take more than one game to fill out this sheet. The more games the scout attends, the more familiar the scout is with the team.

SPOTTING

Spotting is like scouting, but it takes place during the game by spotting trends in the opposition and mistakes with your own team. Spotting should be done from a high vantage point, like the press box if there is one. If possible a telephone or walkie-talkie system can be valuable as the spotter can immediately talk to the players or coach. The scouting charts or any of the other charts discussed may be used by the spotter.

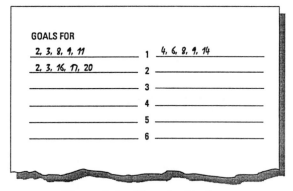

GOALS FOR

2, 3, 8, 9, 11	1	4, 6, 8, 9, 14
2, 3, 16, 17, 20	2	
	3	
	4	
	5	
	6	

Figure 6: Ice Time for Goals

WON		LOST
	1	
	2	
	3	
TOTAL	OT	TOTAL

Figure 7: Face-offs

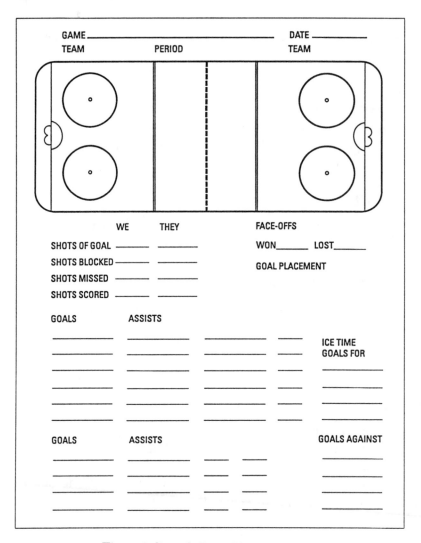

GAME _____ DATE _____
TEAM   PERIOD   TEAM

	WE	THEY
SHOTS OF GOAL	____	____
SHOTS BLOCKED	____	____
SHOTS MISSED	____	____
SHOTS SCORED	____	____

FACE-OFFS

WON _____ LOST _____

GOAL PLACEMENT

GOALS   ASSISTS

ICE TIME
GOALS FOR

GOALS   ASSISTS

GOALS AGAINST

Figure 8: Sample Period Statistics Chart

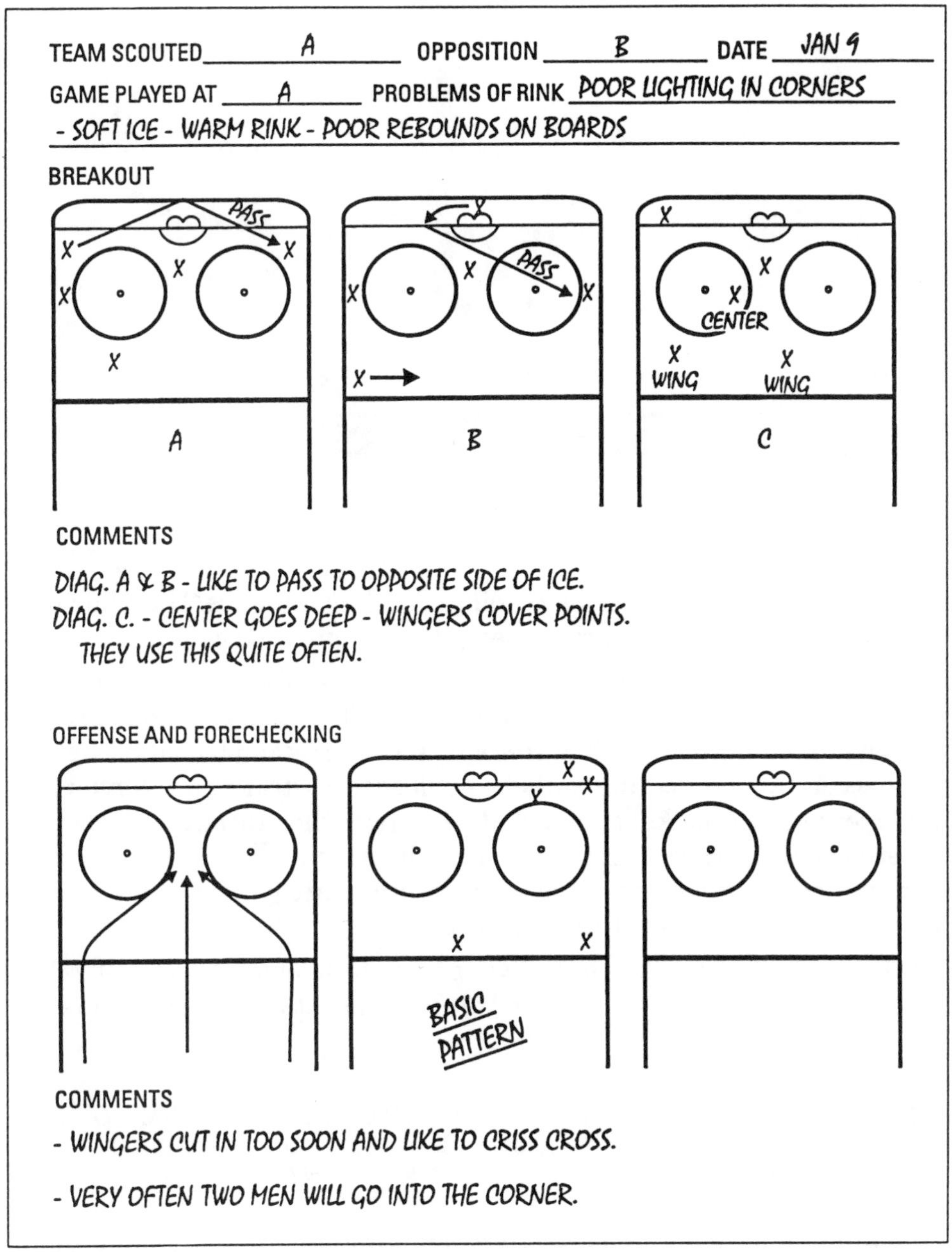

TEAM SCOUTED_____A_____ OPPOSITION _____B_____ DATE __JAN 9__

GAME PLAYED AT _____A_____ PROBLEMS OF RINK __POOR LIGHTING IN CORNERS__

__- SOFT ICE - WARM RINK - POOR REBOUNDS ON BOARDS__

BREAKOUT

A   B   C

COMMENTS

DIAG. A & B - LIKE TO PASS TO OPPOSITE SIDE OF ICE.

DIAG. C. - CENTER GOES DEEP - WINGERS COVER POINTS.
   THEY USE THIS QUITE OFTEN.

OFFENSE AND FORECHECKING

BASIC PATTERN

COMMENTS

- WINGERS CUT IN TOO SOON AND LIKE TO CRISS CROSS.

- VERY OFTEN TWO MEN WILL GO INTO THE CORNER.

Figure 9: Sample Scouting Form

10

STATISTICS

The computer has facilitated the keeping of hockey statistics. The following stats were developed with a spreadsheet. It is extremely easy.

The purpose of keeping individual and team statistics is to monitor performance in relation to the team's objectives. Statistics detect deviations from standards so that the coach can recognize and correct problems. Statistics must be accurate for inaccurate statistics can lead to frustration and confusion. The players should be kept informed as to how the statistics are being registered, why they are getting the values that they are, and why a certain statistic is being kept and how it relates to team strategy. The following are some statistics that the coach may like to use.

GAME STATISTIC FORM. The following form is a sample of the statistics for a single game. Each game is then added to a running total to give a season stat sheet.

NO.	NAME	G	A	PTS	P/M	SH/G	SH%	PA/A	PA/C	PA%	PEN	PIM	TOTAL
3	Fred	1	1	1	0	3	33%	2	1	50%	1	2	16
4	Joe	0	0	0	-1	2	0%	13	8	62%	2	4	-1
5	Bill												

The key to the above chart is: G = GOALS, A = ASSISTS, PTS = POINTS, P/M = GOALS PLUS/MINUS, SH/G = SHOTS ON GOAL, SH% = SCORING PERCENTAGE, PA/A = PASSES ATTEMPTED, PA/C = PASSES COMPLETED, PA% = PASSING PERCENTAGE, PEN = PENALTIES, PIM = PENALTIES IN MINUTES.

The total column is a rating they receive by adding and subtracting the following values. The formula looks like this:

TOTAL = (5 X GOALS) + (10 X ASSISTS) + (5 X GOALS PLUS/MINUS) + (SHOTS ON GOAL) + (PASSES COMPLETED) - (3 X PENALTIES).

These values were chosen to emphasis a passing style of play. The coach in this example wants lots of passes, so he gives 10 points for each assist and one point for each pass completed. The coach is trying to discourage penalties so three points are deducted for each penalty.

FORMULAS

Goals, assists and total points are simple addition.

P/M, the goals plus and minus is for the player on the ice when a goal is scored for the team and when a goal is scored against the team. The formula is "goals for" minus the "goals against." SH/G, the shots on goal, is the number of shots the players has on goal that would have scored if the goaltender was not in the net.

SH%, the shooting and scoring percentage, is determined by the number of goals divided by the number of shots times 100. In the example above Fred scored one goal with three attempted shots.

The formula: $^{G}/_{SH/G}$ X 100 $\qquad$ $^{1}/_{3}$ X 100 = 33%

The SH/G can be switched to SH/A for shots attempted on goal. The following samples used the SH/A.

PA/A and PA/C is passes attempted and passes completed and this is self explanatory.

PA% is the percentage of passes completed. The formula is passes completed divided by passes attempted times 100.

The formula: $^{PC}/_{PA}$ X 100 $\qquad$ for Fred: $^{1}/_{2}$ x 100 = 50%

PEN is the number of penalties while PIM is the number of penalties in minutes.

FORMULAS FOR GOALIES —chart 1 bottom

The GP = games played, PP = periods played, SHT = shots on goal, SVE = saves, GOAL = number of goals scored on the goalie are all self explanatory.

The SV% is the save percentage. The formula is saves divided by the number of shots times 100.

The formula: $^{saves}/_{shots}$ X 100 $\qquad$ $^{1}/_{3}$ X 100 = 33%

The GMA is the average number of goals against the goalie per game (game average). The formula is number of goals divided by the number of games times 100.

The formula: $^{total\,goals}/_{total\,games}$ Chart 1 example: $^7/_1 = 7$

A team shot and passing chart will look like this:

TEAM	DATE	GOOD	BAD	TOTAL	PERCENT
U.W.	DEC. 10				
	SHOTS	20	10	30	66.6 %
	PASSES	150	50	200	75.0 %
U.Z.	DEC. 15				
	SHOTS				
	PASSES				

SEASON AVERAGE TO DATE:
    SHOTS:
    PASSES:

Another interesting statistic is to record the time in each end zone of play. The statistician simply records the time the puck is in each end zone. This statistic will tell the coach were most of his play is occurring and its relationship with the enemy.

Of course keeping a chart of where on the ice the shots are coming from and by what players gives us our ability to determine our players good shots and bad shots.

Charts on goalkeepers should also be devised. A diagram of a goal with the position of each goal scored will help to reveal strength and weakness areas of the goaltender. Also a short record of how the goaltender played each goal scored on him may also be helpful. Actually, a goalkeeper should be keeping a record of each time he gets beat. This can be most helpful for future use.

A computer will also print out excellent graphs on statistics. The following two graphs for passes and shots are easily read and understood. Following the sample charts are the graphs.

Chart 1 is a sample statistic chart for a single game.

Chart 2 is a sample statistic chart for the season to date.

Chart 3 is a sample team passing and shooting chart showing the results for each game.

Chart 4 is an interesting chart and shows how the stats can be manipulated to different effects. This charts takes the players in groups of their lines and defensemen combinations. The four line combinations are the gold line, wine line, red line and green line. The defensemen are grouped to their playing combinations. This chart may give the coach an idea of how the line and defense combinations are doing.

Chart 5 is a graph for passes for the season.

Chart 1: Game Statistics

Name	G	A	PTS	P/M	SH/A	SH%	PA/A	PA/C	PA%	PEN	PIM	TOT
Carmen	0	1	1	0	1	0%	11	3	27%	0	0	14
Floyd	0	0	0	-1	1	0%	24	15	63%	0	0	11
Miller	0	0	0	-1	0	ERR	10	7	70%	0	0	2
Johns	0	0	0	-2	0	ERR	0	0	ERR	0	0	-10
Sticks	0	0	0	-1	1	0%	9	8	89%	2	4	-2
Plied	0	0	0	-1	1	0%	11	7	64%	0	0	-6
Zoff	0	0	0	-2	0	ERR	6	4	67%	0	0	-6
Jermen	0	0	0	-2	2	0%	32	24	75%	0	0	16
Alden	0	0	0	-2	2	9%	10	8	80%	1	2	-3
Grog	0	0	0	-1	0	ERR	6	5	83%	0	0	0
Hall	0	0	0	1	2	0%	8	5	63%	1	0	9
Holly	1	0	1	0	2	50%	9	6	67%	0	0	13
Deback	1	0	1	0	2	59%	7	4	57%	1	2	8
Batts	0	0	0	0	0	ERR	0	0	ERR	0	0	0
Hanni	0	0	0	0	0	ERR	0	0	ERR	0	0	0
Rems	0	0	0	0	0	ERR	0	0	ERR	0	0	0

Key: G = Goals   A = Assists PTS = Points +/− = Goals Plus/Minus SH/G = Shots on Goal SH% = Shooting % $^{PA}/_A$ = Passes Attempted PA% = Passing   PEN = Penalties PIM = Penalties in Minutes TOT = This is a rating score with the following values:

Sum of (5 X Goals) + (10 X Assists) + (5 X Goals Plus/Minus) + (Shots on Goal) + (Passes Completed) − (3 X Penalties)

Key for Goalies: GP = Games Played PP = Periods Played SHT = Shots on Goal SVE = Saves GOAL = Goals Against SV% = Save % GMA = Game Average   W/L/T = Won/Loss/Ties

Goalie	GP	PP	SHT	SVE	GOAL	SV%	GMA	W/L/T
Alots	1	3	42	35	7	83.3%	7	ERR
Smith	0	0	0	0	0	ERR	ERR	R0/4/0
Jones	0	0	0	0	0	ERR	ERR	R0/2/0

Chart 2: Season Statistics

Name	G	A	PTS	P/M	SH/A	SH%	PA/A	PA/C	PA%	PEN	PIM	TOT
Carmen	0	0	0	-16	6	0%	201	133	66%		8	47
Floyd	1	2	3	-14	7	14%	92	51	55%		4	7
Miller	1	1	2	-20	11	9%	222	137	62%		9	51
Johns	0	2	2	-15	10	0%	69	42	61%		8	-15
Sticks	2	0	2	-11	5	40%	58	29	50%		0	-11
Plied	0	0	0	-4	5	0%	48	28	58%		14	-5
Zoff	0	1	1	-13	17	0%	152	106	65%		22	47
Jermen	0	0	0	-15	3	0%	96	62	75%		6	-19
Alden	0	0	0	-24	8	0%	206	136	66%		22	3
Grog	3	1	4	-15	22	14%	97	56	58%		22	10
Hall	0	0	0	-6	0	ERR	21	12	57%		2	-21
Holly	4	2	6	-8	9	44%	114	74	65%		8	71
Deback	1	1	2	-10	15	7%	117	76	65%		8	44
Batts	1	1	2	-12	4	25%	80	54	68%		6	4
Hanni	0	1	1	-10	3	0%	36	14	39%		2	-26
Rems	0	1	1	-9	2	0%	59	34	58%		27	-23

Key:

G = Goals A = Assists PTS = Points P/M = Goals Plus/Minus SH/G = Shots on Goal SH% = Shooting % PA/A = Passes Attempted PA/C = Passes Completed PA% = Passing % PEN = Penalties

TOT = This is a rating score with the following values: Sum of (5 X Goals) + (10 X Assists) + (5 X Goals Plus/Minus) + (Shots on Goal) + (Passes Completed) – (3 X Penalties)

Key for Goalies:

GP = Games Played PP = Periods Played SHT = Shots on Goal SVE = Saves

GOAL = Goals Against SV% = Save % GMA = Game Average W/L/T = Won/Loss/Ties

Goalie	GP	PP	SHT	SVE	GOAL	SV%	GMA	W/L/T
Alots	4	12	256	205	51	80.1%	13	0/4/0
Smith	4	12	263	216	47	82.1%	12	0/4/0
Jones	2	6	98	66	32	67.3%	16	0/2/0

Chart 3: Team Statistics   **State University**   **1992-1993**

Team	Date	Sht/Pas	Good	Bad	Percent	Total
Boston	11/3 (H)	Shots	12	13	48%	25
		Passes	89	23	79%	112
New York	11/14 (H)	Shots	14	6	70%	20
		Passes	72	42	63%	114
Penna	11/24 (H)	Shots	10	10	50%	20
		Passes	119	109	52%	228
St. Aug.	12/2 (H)	Shots	25	9	74%	34
		Passes	106	63	63%	169
Sidells	12/4 (H)	Shots	16	8	67%	24
		Passes	149	66	69%	215
EastState	12/5 (A)	Shots	0	0	ERR	0
		Passes	160	98	62%	258
EastState	12/11 (A)	Shots	20	10	67%	30
		Passes	153	108	59%	261
Boston	12/12 (A)	Shots	0	0	ERR	0
		Passes	171	95	64%	266
U.T.A	12/15 (A)	Shots	16	9	64%	25
		Passes	176	65	73%	241
U.T.A.	12/29 (H)	Shots	22	10	69%	32
		Passes	167	94	64%	261
WestState	12/30 (H)	Shots	32	25	56%	57
		Passes	0	0	ERR	0
Sevelle	1/5 (H)	Shots	24	10	71%	34
		Passes	248	47	84%	295
L.A.State	1/15 (H)	Shots	36	11	78%	80
		Passes	217	29	88%	246
L.A.State	1/16 (H)	Shots	62	18	78%	80
		Passes	205	60	77%	265

Chart 4: State University Unit Scores 1992-1993
Boston Series January 15 & 16

Name	G	A	PTS	+/-	SH/A	SH%	PA/A	PA/C	PA%	PEN	PIM	TOT
Gold	2	1	3	-1	35	6%	158	132	84%	3	6	173
Wall	0	0	0	-1	11	0%	61	55	90%	1	2	58
Caper	1	1	2	-1	18	6%	52	40	77%	1	2	65
Blake	1	0	1	-1	6	17%	45	37	82%	1	2	40
Red	3	1	4	-1	16	19%	132	114	86%	3	14	141
Carmen	1	1	2	-1	3	33%	46	40	87%	0	0	53
Floyd	0	0	0	-1	5	0%	40	36	90%	1	2	33
Miller	2	0	2	-1	8	25%	46	38	83%	2	12	45
White	1	1	2	0	14	7%	113	90	80%	3	6	110
Johns	0	0	0	0	3	0%	23	19	83%	0	0	22
Sticks	0	1	1	0	2	0%	17	16	94%	1	2	25
Plied	1	0	1	0	9	11%	73	55	75%	2	4	63
Green	1	0	1	2	1	100%	7	7	100%	1	2	20
Zoff	0	0	0	0	0	ERR	0	0	ERR	0	0	0
Jermen	1	0	1	2	1	100%	6	6	100%	1	2	19
Alden	0	0	0	0	0	ERR	1	1	100%	0	0	1
Grog/Hall	1	0	1	2	1	7%	219	187	85%	1	2	239
Grog	0	0	0	2	7	0%	103	90	87%	1	2	104
Hall	1	2	3	4	8	13%	116	97	84%	0	1	150
Hol/Deb/Ba	0	0	0	-3	7	0%	91	71	78%	0	0	63
Holly	0	0	0	-4	3	0%	54	38	70%	0	0	21
Deback	0	0	0	0	0	ERR	0	0	ERR	0	0	0
Batts	0	0	0	-2	4	0%	37	33	89%	0	0	27
Han/Rem	0	0	0	0	9	0%	111	86	77%	4	8	83
Hanni	0	0	0	0	4	0%	58	46	79%	3	6	41
Rems	0	0	0	0	5	0%	53	40	75%	1	2	42

Key:

G = Goals   A = Assists   PTS = Points   +/- = Goals Plus/Minus   Sh/G = Shots on Goal SH% = Shooting PA/A = Passes Attempted PA/C = Passes Completed PA% = Passing % PEN = Penalties PIM = Penalties in Minutes TOT = This is a rating score with the following values: Sum of (5 X Goals) + (10 X Assists) + (5 X Goals Plus/Minus) + (Shots on Goal) + (Passes Completed) – (3 X Penalties)

Key for Goalies:

GP = Games Played PP = Periods Played SHT = Shots on Goal Sve = Saves GOAL = Goals Against SV% = Save % GMA = Game Average

Goalie	GP	PP	SHT	SVE	GOALS	V%	GMA
Alots	1	3	40	33	7	82.5%	7
Smith	1	3	36	32	4	88.9%	4
Jones	0	0	0	0	0	ERR	ERR

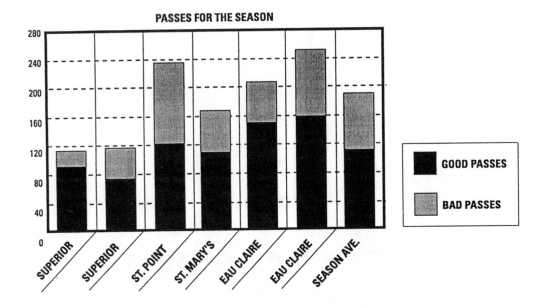

Chart 5: Passes for the Season

11

INJURIES AND MEDICAL PROBLEMS

Injuries will occur even though excellent preventive measures are taken. A competent coach must know how to handle the injury when it occurs. He should know a little first aid, but he must also be aware of his own limitations and responsibilities: he is, after all, a coach, not a doctor. In most instances, medical help should be used. Consulting a doctor will often take the burden of responsibility off the coach and transfer it to one who is qualified to diagnose and treat the injury.

Injuries and medical problems should be considered from four points of view: prevention, diagnosis, treatment and rehabilitation.

PREVENTION

Strength and flexibility of the athlete are two of the most important factors in preventing an injury. The poorly conditioned athlete puts his muscles in an overtaxed state and thus becomes highly susceptible to strains and sprains. The more an athlete forces his muscles to go beyond his strength and flexibility level, the greater the potential for injury. Therefore, the higher the strength and flexibility level the athlete can achieve, the less chance for injury.

Diet

Participation in sports requires energy. Since energy comes from food, the athlete must eat a balanced diet. Such a diet should include proteins, fats, carbohydrates, vitamins, minerals and water in proper proportions. A good diet will eliminate the need for pills and vitamins. The basic athletic diet consists mostly of carbohydrates for energy. The proteins repair torn tissue and the fats do provide some energy but not as quickly as the carbohydrates. The body requires about 60-70% carbohydrates, 20-30% fats and 10-20% proteins. A coach in youth hockey will have little chance to influence the diets of the players. About all he can do is make his players aware of eating properly and hope the parents will help.

An athlete who has been eating well and regularly will be more alert and ready to participate in activity without undue fatigue. The athlete who tires easily because of poor diet, inadequate rest, or poor conditioning puts himself at a high risk for injury.

Equipment

Equipment is also very important in the prevention of injuries. A player must be adequately protected with properly fitted equipment before going into the rink. He should not have to assume the risk of injury because of poor equipment.

Coaching & Good Officiating

Good coaching can also help prevent injuries. One example would be making proper line changes during a game help to prevent the tired player from overtaxing his muscles. Progressive development of the player's skills will also help the player play correctly and more safely.

Good officiating is another factor in injury prevention as the officials can keep the game under control and stop play as danger and illegal tactics develop.

Regular Medical Exams

It should be mandatory for all athletes to have a medical examination before being eligible to play or practice. The coach, school athletic director, or the team organization should have a medical record of each player. The medical record will provide a doctor with the player's history in the event treatment is needed. An example of the necessity for a player's medical history would be a player that is allergic to penicillin. The coach would have no way of knowing about the player's allergy, and the consequences could be very serious indeed.

DIAGNOSIS

Some injuries are simple and can be treated by a coach or trainer if the treatment is uncomplicated. In making a diagnosis, the coach must be aware that many injuries are complicated and obscure from immediate or first diagnosis. A good example of this is referred pain which is difficult to evaluate because it is distant from the actual sight of the injury. Some injuries are latent in that they do not show up until well after the injury has occurred. Medical attention within twenty-four hours is neccessary in the diagnosis and treatment of most injuries and helps prevent further damage or re-injury.

BASIC TREATMENT

Primary rules in injury treatment are:

W = Wrap: wrap or compress the injury.

R = Rest: rest the affected part — immobilize if necessary.

E = Elevate: if possible the affected part should be raised slightly when resting.

C = Cold: all injuries should be treated with cold treatments.

If you take the first letter on each of the treatments, W, R, E, C, we get the work WREC as a means to help remember the treatment.

Some trainers prefer the word RICE which means the same as WREC.

R = Rest

I = Ice (cold)

C = Compress (wrap)

E = Elevate

The application of cold will help to reduce swelling and pain in the injured area; cold treatments should be applied immediately to the injury to prevent swelling. At no time should heat be applied to an injury before the passage of a minimum of forty-eight hours, and such treatment should be given as recommended by a doctor. During the first forty-eight hour period, cold treatments should be given for twenty minutes every four hours.

Cold treatments and cold packs are terms used in the application of cold to an injury. A wet towel wrapped around snow or ice will produce an excellent cold pack. A frozen, water soaked sponge also works very well. When applied, the frozen sponge will soon take on the contours of the injured area and give an excellent fit. Commercial cold packs are good for instant use and when away from easy access to ice.

REHABILITATION

The rehabilitation of injuries is the most crucial consideration in their management and it requires experienced judgment and knowledge of the activity in which the person is to participate. The coach and medical staff should consult closely in gradually reconditioning the treated athlete to maximum fitness before permitting full participation. Special protective strapping, padding or guards may assist in the early return to a full performance.

SOME BASIC GUIDELINES

Whenever there is a chance of injury, physical or mental harm and the need for first-aid, a coach must be aware of liability problems. The following guidelines may be of help in preventing liability law suites.

Remain Calm. Remain calm so that you can present an image of being in control. By being calm, the thought process can be organized and accurate. Anxiety and pressure affect not only the players but also the coach.

Never Assume the Role of a Physician. Put the responsibility of diagnosis on a physician who is qualified to make such decisions. Unless you are a doctor, you haven't been trained to diagnose medical problems.

Never Do Anything that Could be Interpreted as Gross Negligence. Remember, as a coach you have assumed responsibility for the care of your players. Do not be negligent. Supervise all activities.

Never Move a Player with a Suspected Serious Injury. This means do not sit him up, roll him over, straighten his legs, etc. Leave the movement to qualified people.

Do Not Take Chances with the Hope Nothing May Happen. Use good judgement making decisions.

Do Not Play the Game if Serious Injury is Possible to a Player or Team. Safety is a must. Regularly inspect equipment and facilities.

Never Play a Player After a Serious Injury or Suspected Serious Injury. Some injuries are latent and take effect after the incident. Sometimes the extra physical effort after an injury will magnify the injury to permanent damage. Head injuries have caused death while playing well after the incident.

Section 4

Communications

Coaching is communications. The coach is always communicating with the team, management and fans. In many cases even with the parents. Messages, directives, orders, demands, encouragement, praise, etc., must be given in clear and precise manners. There must be no misunderstandings. Knowing when to praise, encourage, reprimand is important. Timing of communications is important as is the intensity of the message. There is a time to be mad and a time to be calm and time for various stages between the two extremes. Good and effective communications know when and how.

12

COMMUNICATIONS

It goes without saying that communication is one of the most important aspects of coaching. The players and coach must communicate freely and easily at all times. Communications going both ways must be understood exactly by each so that no misinterpretation of the message is possible. Misinterpreted messages can lead to needless disaster. The following are some guidelines that may be of help.

BREVITY: Keep your messages brief. If necessary, break the message down into parts. Work on one part and then work on the other part. There is no limit to the number of parts for the total picture. Just keep each part short and understandable.

THE OBJECTIVE: The objective or what you want to say should be clear cut and precise. No hidden meanings or exaggerations. Be certain of your objective in the event you have to defend your message.

INFORMATION: Know and assemble all your facts, good and bad, when determining your objective. Your facts must be accurate as your message is only as accurate as the facts. In gathering information, the following words may be of help in making your message as clear as possible: who, when, where, what, why, and how.

THE TARGET: Who is the message for? A player? A trainer? The manager? Target your message to the person responsible for carrying out the request. Do not give someone else a message to tell your intended receiver unless it is a last resort. Face to face confrontation is best.

KNOW YOUR TARGET: It is important to know your target. Some players communicate differently than others. Some think differently than others. Know your target and then give the message to him in terms that are understandable to him. Talk his language.

INTEREST: Although it is not possible at all times, try to keep your communications interesting. Salesmen use the term "hook" as a means of grabbing the persons interest and attention. A short statement that gains the players full attention is a powerful message.

FOLLOW-THROUGH: When the message is conveyed, follow-through with the closing. The closing will take various styles of action. If the message is about the wingers staying wide, make sure the wingers are staying wide. Never give the message and then let it ride hoping the effect will happen or take care of itself.

PICTURES: Good messages or instructions carry a vivid picture of exactly what it is that you wish to accomplish. Although the message is in words the receiving of the message is a picture. A picture is often easier to follow and understand, and a good picture is remembered longer.

HOW YA' SAY IT: It is not so much what you say as how you say it. Give your message with belief and commitment. Use no hesitancy in your speech. Speak with energy and vitality. Be convincing by showing honesty and integrity. Try not to make your messages dictatorial. Smile if the situation presents itself.

OR ELSE: Never give a message with a "or else" statement at the end. Coaches have said "Do this or else," and, when challenged, have no come back. Many coaches have been backed up to the wall when someone returns the comment "or else what?" If it ever happens to you, it may be best to simply just laugh it off with the team and enjoy the humor.

BODY LANGUAGE: Back up your words with the correct body language. This was discussed earlier, but it is worth mentioning again.

SPEECHES: Often coaches are called upon to speak to groups or clubs. Some important communications are:

1. Never memorize your speech. This is dull and boring to the audience. Learn your speech, master it, but never memorize it word for word.

2. Never read the speech. Talk to your audience. Tell them what's up or happening. Free wheel it.

3. If you need notes for a speech then highlight or mark the key words so that a quick glance will tell you where you are in the speech and help you to keep the order and continuity going.

4. Use the guidelines of communications previously mentioned. Especially the brevity, the target or type of audience, the objective. If you are good at it use humor, if not forget it, it may unexpectedly come anyway. There is nothing worse than someone trying to be funny. Funny people do not try, they are funny.

5. When you speak look human and act human. Be natural. Do not try to be formal, staid or a piece of granite.

6. Look at your audience. There is nothing sincere about a speaker looking above or around the audience. Look 'em in the eye.

7. Do not make distracting moves or sounds when speaking. Some speakers are annoying to listen to as they talk and jingle the change in their pockets. Some crumple and fold their notes. Have a good beginning, a good ending and keep it short and simple in between.

8. It's an old trick but it works: practice your speech in front of the mirror.

QUESTIONS: Coaches often are confronted with questions. Many coaches fear these sessions because they feel they may not have the answers. Coaches should look upon these questions as an opportunity to get their point across and clear up any misconceptions.

TELEPHONES: The telephone is a fast and modern method of communications. Unfortunately, many people cannot convey their message over the phone quickly and accurately. So many phone messages are confusing. When using the phone, get organized and state your case efficiently. "humms" and "ahhs" and "do you know what I mean" are irritating to the listener.

MEETINGS: Team meetings or staff meetings are often too long, too boring, or too frequent. Keep your meeting short and to the point. Solve the problem. Do not belabor the problem. Have meetings only when necessary and make them interesting.

PAPER COMMUNICATIONS: When communicating on paper or with words, the above principles still apply. Brevity, clarity, objectivity, understandability, information and targeting the message are still paramount to the paper message.

13

UNDERSTANDING THE TEAM THROUGH ITS HUMOR

Humor is the fun part of life. We treat it lightly, but humor is serious and very complex. There is meaning in humor. Sometimes the message is coded or hidden and is difficult to analyze, but it can be helpful in understanding team dynamics.

Athletes are fun-loving people. They have a strong play attitude developed from childhood. Research has found that the humorous child has high levels of physical energy with an intense interest in gross motor skills. As the child progresses to higher levels of play and age groups, he brings with him not only his playing skills, but also his humor skills.

There are three types of comics. A team may have all three types or fewer.

The FOOL is low on the comic scale. He is simply foolish and unintelligent. He is confusion, the scapegoat, the butt of jokes. He is unaware of his humor.

The CLOWN is above the fool but along the same lines. He is aware of his antics. The fool and clown both may put their jerseys on backwards but the fool is unaware of doing this while the clown is doing it on purpose to create humor. The clown walks a thin line of humor and rejection. If his humor is unsuccessful he does not become accepted by the team.

The WIT is the highest in status. His humor is cognitive and intelligent. He has power in the group and is very often a leader. If the wit's style is sarcastic, derogatory or destructive he may lose status and power. If he does not lose status, his negative style of humor may split the team. If the wit's negativism is directed at the coach or administration, then loyalty, discipline, and team cohesion may be in jeopardy.

Locker room humor is a joking relationship of blasphemy, cursing, obscenities, insults and antagonisms. It is the familiarity of the group members that create "in humor", a type of humor that is understood by the group. It is not unusual for outsiders to not understand what is so funny; they are not familiar with the circumstances that create the humor. "In humor" often leads to a bonding of the in-members as they have knowledge of things the outsiders lack. Sometimes the coach may be an outsider to some of the "in humor" of the players. "In humor" is a code that can only be translated by the in-group. Many times "in humor" does not take place with an outsider present. Sometimes there is no problem as outsiders do not understand anyway. New players often feel left out in the team frolicking as they have not lived through the past experiences that developed the code. In time, the new players will learn the humor and become a part of the humor if they are accepted by the team. Although new members of the team may be introduced to the team in formal or informal circumstances, the new players do not feel part of the team until they are part of the team humor. As the new players are teased, joked and played with, their team bonding increases as does their positive feelings for the team. Players who are not part of team humor feel alienated from the group.

Group familiarity breeds nicknames and nicknames are often a humorous form of labeling an athlete. "Butterfingers," "animal," etc. are often portrayals, or extreme contradictions of the player. Often the labeled nickname is not understood by the outsider but it has deep meaning to the group or team. Nicknames, a form of "in humor," are a means of expressing acceptance of a player to the group. When new players are given a nickname, they become a part of the team.

A player's status will often fluctuate with his present playing accomplishments. Playing well means higher status and playing bad is lower status. A high status player when playing bad must be careful with his humor. His power is gone so the message is received differently. A low status player playing very well can say things that he would not or should not say when he was low on the scale.

It has been found that veterans often use humor to impose values on rookies and new players. The rookies and younger players use humor for self-protection to cover up their mistakes and inadequacies.

Team comedians are often a source of irritation to the coach. The coach must analyze team humor for the message. Maybe it is not so bad. Perhaps the coach is just humor fatigued. The coach must be careful in how he deals with this type of problem. Destroying a comic or cutting the comic from the team may destroy team humor and fun and as a result team unity and harmony may be affected. If the comics humor is not negative or destructive he may be of value to the team. Tread softly . . . but carry a big stick.

If the comic becomes too burdened with team responsibilities, he may see this as taking away his fun time. If this new role of responsibility changes the comic's positive humor to sarcastic and negative humor then a message is clear that he wants his old ways. The team also needs his old ways. You do not want a leader with sarcastic and negative humor. Such humor is too destructive to team dynamics.

It is part of the comic's personality to have difficulty with team rules and discipline. However, the comic needs the team for an audience and for his play time. This factor can keep the comic in line although it may be difficult.

Humor can help team cohesion or it can develop team conflict. Positive humor can bind the group together. Negative humor will tear the team apart and develop cliques. Negative humor directed to another team can bind the team. Cliques target humor to other cliques or teammates as a means of strengthening their position in the group.

The team scapegoat or fool/clown can be valuable to the team by absorbing the negative and hostile humor of a team. Such a person allows the players to vent their anger within the group with no fear of retaliation or disruption by the scapegoat or fool. Scapegoats are excellent and easy targets. Teams with no scapegoat may use the coach as a scapegoat. For this reason, a good team scapegoat may be a valuable asset and well worth keeping on the team.

Jocular griping is a form of humorous complaining and may be a camouflage for light hostility. This may also be a forewarning of possible problems. The coach must read the situation carefully as there is usually a strong message trying to be conveyed through jocular or humorous griping.

Players with an internal locus of control feel personally responsible for the outcome of events. Such people feel that the loss of a game is their own responsibility and a result of their own mistakes. These players are more team oriented, humorous and easier to coach. The external locus of control players believe that outside agencies like luck, weather, etc. affect the outcome of events. These players are less humorous and suffer from anxiety and depression more than the internals. Naturally, externals are more difficult to coach.

Coaches should be aware of changes in humor on a group level and in the individuals. Very often the signs of depression or a troubled mind is the lack of humor. Whenever a player loses his sense of humor then it is very likely he may be having problems. Everyone has bad days and on these days they may fail to see the humor around them. This is usually no concern for alarm; however, if the loss of humor seems prolonged then check it out.

The analysis of humor is difficult and takes practice. If the coach is aware that humor has a message of positive and/or negative value then a foundation is established for its understanding. One must be careful to not over-read the situation. One joke does not a trend make. Look for trends and actions that back up the humor analysis.

Section 5

Leadership

A great hockey team must have strong leadership, from the top management, the coach, the captains, and even the players. On good teams, everyone plays his role effectively. The coach leads, the players follow. Good leadership will also help in developing team spirit and team unity — a cohesion — of the players, team, and organization.

14

LEADERSHIP

Leaders determine the future.

Coaches are leaders. Leaders get people to follow and achieve new and higher levels. Leadership assists the followers in developing their potential. This is the essence of coaching.

The following strategies work for most leaders; however, it must be stated that some strategies do not apply to some personalities and situations. Just because a strategy worked for one person is no guarantee it will work for another. Different personalities of the leader and the group may result in the use of variations to a strategy. Good leaders know their followers' personalities and how they interact with his personality. Humor is a good example of the various benefits of a strategy. Humor can be used by a leader with tremendous efficiency, if it fits his style. Humor by some leaders may be interpreted by his followers as a lack of dedication and seriousness to the situation. In a similar situation with two different teams, one coach may be able to use humor effectively while another coach may use the same humor and create antagonism and resentment.

PHILOSOPHY

A coach must have a philosophy for life and a philosophy for coaching. The two are very compatible. A philosophy is needed to give consistent direction to the coach and the players. Weak coaches have inconsistent philosophies or no philosophy and as a result their teams lack direction and purpose. Lack of direction and purpose shows itself as the pressure increases. Players in this situation have no criteria to guide them in their behavior on and off the ice. Players know exactly where they stand when under the guidance of a strong philosophy. A consistent philosophy helps to firmly establish and remove uncertainty of training rules, playing strategy, discipline, and team goals.

WINNING/PERFORMANCE

Coaches become so concerned about winning that they lose perspective after a loss. Losses will happen, try to learn from them. Good coaches work on performance and execution of mental and physical skills. Perform well and winning will follow. Players and teams when competing above their level of ability may not win, but they can be expected to perform to the best of their ability. The good and great coaches never tell their players that they must win the game. Their practice sessions and pregame talks do not emphasize winning. The emphasis of winning is just putting more pressure on the athlete. The lead-up to the game is on performance and execution; if these goals are met, winning will take care of itself.

PREJUDICE

A coach must not fall victim to prejudice of people and/or ideas. Good coaches are continually open minded. Looking for new ways, new ideas, and new ways of looking at things. The authors have found excellent success by talking to people who never saw a hockey game before. Their interpretation of the game is often quite different from the avid fan or participant. Many ideas have come from coaches of other sports as they see hockey through the eyes of their sport. Many ideas of strategy have come through discussions with basketball, soccer, and lacrosse coaches. Mental strategies and philosophies have come from golf and tennis. Football coaches are excellent teachers on coaching organization, preparations and planning. There is a world of knowledge out there in the other sports. Use it.

BEING OPEN

Coaches should be open, aware and less judgmental when dealing with their players. Sometimes being open and receptive is taken as being naive or even gullible, but in the long run it is the best strategy. Such action is necessary to develop trust. Jumping to critical solutions can develop a lack of trust with the players. When the lack of trust develops, communications just get worse and worse as deceit between player and coach grows. Coaches and players must communicate with each other and among themselves. Trust must prevail.

Being flexible is a form of being open. At times the coach must bend and "go with the flow." Being flexible does not mean being willing to break. Being flexible means being strong and solid with some give. Good coaches are able to bend without losing face. In fact, the best coaches set up policies so that they can bend if needed with no detrimental effects to the leadership. Every problem has extenuating circumstances. Good leaders are aware of this and even prepared for such eventual circumstances.

SELFISHNESS

Good coaches provide a service to the team. The good coach places the well being of the team above his own ego. Many coaches are in the game for their own glory. Their players are not humans but robots. Selfish coaches stand on shaky ground. Great coaches give the glory and credit to the players. Humble but confident, the best coaches provide leadership to the team.

The coach must be without ego. The coach must not believe he is above all others. If the coach is ego-centered, the players will soon fail to follow. Coaches with overdeveloped egos are contradictions in that they preach team unity, working and sharing for the team and yet they selfishly use the team to build their own egos. Players soon recognize this contradiction. Conflict, lack or respect, failure to follow and/or a desire to build their own egos will develop in the players. If a coach wants his players to share in the glory with each other then he must also share with the players.

Coaches must not take the game as a personal confrontation. The purpose of sports is not to determine who is the best coach. Often coaches take the approach to the game that when the team wins, it is the coach's victory; when the team loses, it is the players' loss. Remember that winning and losing are results, not processes. Good coaching is a process. The process of development. Study, analyze and teach the process. Winning will come. Winning isn't everything, but making the effort to is.

TIME TO REFLECT

Coaches must provide their players with time to reflect and digest their learning and performances. Too often the coaches keep pushing the knowledge and performance to the point of weakness. Too much in too little time. When players have time to reflect, they have time to get organized not only physically but mentally. Earlier we discussed reminiscence, whereby the athlete comes back better after some time off. Usually what happens is that the athlete has time to reflect on his performance with the team performance. Things become clearer in the mind. The abstract becomes concrete. Confusion fades away.

Sometimes hockey players have difficulty with an attacking strategy. Continual practice does not always solve the problem. The player is looking at the situation at ice level. Sometimes this player should miss a practice or game and study the situation from high up in the stands or press box. Often this view gives another perspective to the situation as the player is able to see the big picture.

The coach must not only give the players time to reflect and digest, but he must also give himself time to reflect and digest the coaching process. The coach must analyze his data from all perspectives and view points. How do the players interpret the situation? How do the fans see the situation? What about the press? The mental strategies outlined in this book for the players also apply to the coaches. Meditation can be helpful to the coach in letting him reflect and digest the events on the ice. Meditation can help him relax and analyze with a clear mind.

LISTEN

If you cannot feel or see what is happening — listen. Two valuable tools of the coach are his eyes and ears. Look and listen. Be calm and have patience. Stand back and look at the situation from another angle. Pushing too hard for a solution that later proves to be wrong can lead to disharmony. Be calm so that the mind processes the data accurately. Remember, it is not enough to have the facts, the facts must be interpreted correctly. Too often coaches, rushing to solutions, simply misinterpret or do not read the facts correctly.

INTERVENTION

Coaches should not intervene unnecessarily. There is a time to intervene and a time to stay on the sidelines. Intervention, when it is not needed or wanted, can cause problems with the players. Some solutions are best when arrived at by the players themselves. Players give more respect to a coach who lets the players have their freedom. Players do not need the "big brother syndrome" from a coach. A coach must learn when to listen, when to act and when to withdraw. Such skills are difficult to develop, but very effective when implemented.

Some coaches are so self-centered that they think they must make all decision for all the players. Such coaches think they are omnipotent. They don't trust their players to think for themselves. Too much intervention by the coach will spoil the group. Some coaches feel that the only way to be part of the group is to force the group to accept his authority. He forces his decisions through the use of fear. Fear of the coach is his survival. Success can be achieved by this method. The results may not always be favorable as the coach may be disliked, despised, and ridiculed. Often the feared coach's tenure is short lived with his team. In a short period of time, he may move to another group of players where his style will survive for another short term.

OVERKILL

The coach who understands team dynamics will use as little force as possible to get the job done. By using as little force as needed, the coach is able to save the use of increased force for more important and vital situations. Do not use overkill. Save it. Bringing excessive force or overkill to the situation creates conflict and arguments. The atmosphere becomes hostile and lacking in trust and harmony. Players may challenge the coach's authority. This may result in the team splitting into cliques or dissenting groups.

STRONG FORCE

There will come times when the coach must step in with strong force. At the right time, it is needed. Good leaders know when the right time requires action. Analysis and feel, a "gut feeling" often gives the coach his clue for action. Experience will teach timing. Even though strong force is needed, remember that the use of such force will create injury to someone. Someone will be hurt or may feel violated through the force. The repercussions may not show immediately but may reveal themselves later in the season or even in future years. Players do not forget their treatment. It is important to remember that when force is used — do not make it personal. Personal attacks are dangerous and have a way of coming back to haunt the attacker.

CENTERED

Good coaches are centered. They are stable and well balanced. Their emotions are balanced between being high and being low. Their ideas are centered from being too far to the right and too far to the left. In some cases it may be necessary to deviate to the extreme, but care and prudence are necessary. Too far to an extreme creates difficulty in proper evaluations. Stay in the middle and stay centered so that both sides can be evaluated. Centering helps the decision making process.

Attacks and criticisms should be handled in a responsible manner. Coaches who are centered are able to share insight into the problem and solve the problem. Encounters are not necessarily personal or a threat to the ego. Respond to all encounters with necessary action. Do not take some encounters as insignificant and do not overreact to others. Maintain balance. When resolving an encounter, a good leader will always let the opposition save face. Humiliation of the opposition always has repercussions. Never back the opposition into the corner with no escape. This is difficult but respect of the opposition must always be there, if not for this moment, for future encounters.

Good coaches have respect for every encounter and every person associated with that encounter.

BEGINNINGS

Coaches must learn to see the beginning and later stages of development. This is also an awareness of the process of learning. Coaches must learn to recognize problems as they begin so corrective measures may be taken before such measures become to serious and cause conflict in the settlement.

UNITY

Unity is difficult to explain, but it is a necessary development of the coaching process. Teams that have unity of purpose are directed together. Rules and regulations are not needed to keep the players in line and moving to their goals. The players look after each other and help each other. They do not deceive each other. The team and coach are one, a single unit, a team.

KEEP IT SIMPLE

Look for simple solutions first. The solution is often there right in front of our eyes and we often fail to see it. We look in all directions, analyze and look to complex solutions. We become swept up by the excitement and the drama of the moment. Our emotions can influence our decisions and the decision making process.

Even though we stress keeping things simple, the coach must still look at the situation forwards, backwards, inside-out, upside-down, and while it's spinning. Study the situation thoroughly, but look to the core first.

The secrets of leadership seem to be the common sense of simple rules. This may be true but in actual practice and the stress of competition it is not necessarily so. Even in practice, common sense does not always prevail. It is often ignored or forgotten. Complex situations do not necessarily mean complex solutions. Success is often simply carrying out the duties of the position.

THE OBVIOUS

Many times the solutions to problems seem obvious. The obvious is often a deception. Coaches encounter this often. The obvious is often a cover to the real problem. Learn to peek under the obvious.

Very often players will come to the coach to discuss a problem and ask various questions on the subject but not directly related to the problem. This technique is the feeling out process. The player is feeling out the coach to get up the nerve to ask the question or feeling out the coach to see if the coach is receptive toward the player and his problem. This technique is very common in college, high school and lower levels. Often, this approach lessens as the athlete becomes older, but do not count on it. The coach should always be aware of this situation as an unconcerned attitude may unknowingly be turning the player away. Very often these problems may not seem serious to the coach, but to the player these problems are very serious. Many times these problems are not related to hockey, but are personal.

POWER

A wise leader must never be self-centered. The leader must provide service to the team, players, and management. This is were power of the coach lies. The coach that gives wise leadership through his service to the team receives power to his position from the players. Power is not taken from the players, nor is it granted by the position. Power is earned from the players through cooperation, mutual respect and sharing. Power that is demanded without being earned or through the position, is shaky and weak. Shaky and weak power does not hold up when the pressure is on.

Leaders must never abuse their power. They must never demand more than is required to meet the goal. Overkill is not always necessary. Handle power with respect and the double edged sword that it is. Abuse of power will lead to rebellion within the team.

LEADER FOLLOWING

Leaders must learn how things happen. By learning how things happen the leader must follow. A leader following seems like a contradiction, fortunately it is not. The wise leader learns all aspects of the group. As earlier discussed the coach looks at the group sideways, forward, backwards, upside-down and inside-out. He leads the group and he follows the group. He learns the group.

AWARENESS

The coach must not only be aware of what is happening to the group but must also be aware of himself and his process with the group. A coach who is aware of his own process of awareness is better able to understand the group process. This understanding will help the coach to decide on action or silence, intervention or withdraw. The aware coach is able to facilitate the team process and help to move it in the desired direction.

TENACITY

Good coaches work through discouragement, apathy, rejection, disappointment and other problems. Weak coaches function well when everything is going their way. Weak coaches do not hold up to adversity. Good coaches persist in leadership and follow-through with their leadership. They do not "jump ship" on the team. They experience joy, laughter, and sadness with their players.

ACCOUNTABILITY

Whether coaches like it or not, they must be held accountable for their actions. This is accepted and should be understood when the job is taken. No coach or leader is beyond approach.

LOYALTY

Leaders must have loyalty to the team, management, school or city they may represent. Lack of loyalty shows a lack of respect and a selfish attitude. A coach should dismiss captains or other players who lack loyalty. Management should dismiss a coach for lack of loyalty. Lack of loyalty can spread throughout the team and management and must never be tolerated.

Disagreements do not necessarily mean lack of loyalty. Handling disagreements is like handling encounters as previously mentioned. Disagreements can present alternative solutions to problems. Disagreements can lead to compromises and a possible better solution. Wise leaders know the difference between disagreements and lack of loyalty. Wise coaches never let disagreements divide the team.

SACRIFICE

Coaches must be willing to make thankless and unwilling sacrifices. Sweat dominates inspiration. Coaching requires work, hard work and lots of it. Most of the work and effort is unrecognized, and at times even annoying, but hard work can be fun.

DISCIPLINE AND MORALE

Discipline and morale will show themselves on the ice and in high-pressure situations. When things are going well, discipline and morale are not a problem. Everyone is happy and functioning efficiently. When the moment is tense and the opposition unrelenting does the team, the individuals and the coach hold up? Yes.

RESPONSIBILITY

The coach must accept his position seriously and be responsible for the duties of the position. Being a coach is a privilege and not a right. The coach must never carry out his duties to the disadvantage of his players. Good coaches do not take more privilege than the players are willing to give. The coach works for the players.

Leaders are responsible for their own actions. What they say they must do. They cannot say one thing and do another. Such action is interpreted by the players as deception. The coach is perceived as devious. Weak coaches avoid responsibility while the great ones accept it.

RESPECT

Coaches should pay courtesy and respect to their subordinate leaders and players. Coaches who cannot give respect cannot earn respect. It is that simple.

ASSISTANT COACHES

Many coaches are weak in utilizing assistant coaches. If you hired an assistant coach then he must have the ability to carry out assigned duties. The coach must trust his subordinates and help in their development to be future coaches and leaders. Assistant coaches, when carrying out a delegated responsibility, must be held accountable for their actions and results.

Weak coaches surround themselves with weak assistants. Weak assistants have problems carrying out responsibilities. Good coaches hire good assistants. Good leadership means good teams.

Strong coaches will also have strong weaknesses. The wise coach will hire assistants to strengthen his weaknesses. The wise coach hires or develops leaders to cover all areas of responsibilities for the team. This way all areas have strong leadership.

DECISIVENESS

Good coaches are decisive. They make decisions and they make them at the right time. Indecisive coaches are doomed to failure. Delays in the decision making process often lead to a lack of uncertainty as to the course of direction. This is readily noticeable by the players who in turn develop a lack of confidence in the leadership.

Coaches must allow their assistants to make decisions to their level of responsibility. This is also a part of the delegation of responsibility. It is also a part of the responsibility of developing future leaders and coaches.

REWARDS

Never reward anyone for doing less than expected. This cheapens the reward and the reward loses its value. Rewards must be earned at the high standard expected. Concern on the use of rewards, verbal or materialistic rewards, should be well considered lest the recipients become reward conscious by acting only for the reward or the recognition. The coaches main concern is the rewarding of his team and not the rewarding of himself. Small rewards like gratitude, concern, interest, and help are often the greatest rewards a coach can make on his players.

DEFEATS

Game defeats and mental defeats will plague the coach. This is to be expected. It goes with the job. Confidence, esteem, and other depressing emotions are normal happenings but they must be of short duration. Grieve —but make it short. A game does not a season make. There is work to be done. A lesson to be learned. Defeat can be a great teacher if it is used to enhance the future. Remember, leaders determine the future. Do not let a temporary defeat slow, stop, or kill you.

ACADEMICS

Many coaches coach players who are attending school. Athletics and academics is still the big question and problem. We will not discuss it here. Players who have school work and athletic work must put the two together. No priorities should be needed. The player has a responsibility to do both his academics and athletics at the highest level possible. Often players will shift priorities to meet his feelings at the time. Often players will use priorities as a scapegoat or a rationalizing process. An example would be to say "I cannot practice today because I have to do a term paper for tomorrow, after all academics comes first." Well, the facts are correct but the reasoning is wrong. The player should have been working on his term paper earlier and not left it for the last day. This requires planning and it is the players responsibility to plan and prepare accordingly. If something should come up that the player may have to miss practice then the coach should be notified prior to practice so plans can be arranged or changed. Hockey is a team game and a missing player alters the team practice.

MOTIVATION

Is motivation the coach's responsibility? To some extent it may be but it is also the player's responsibility to motivate himself. If the athlete is not motivated to play and practice then maybe he should not be playing the game. Good coaching will help the players maintain their high level of motivation. Weak and poor coach's stifle and kill the athlete's motivation. Motivation is often directly related to the quality of the coaching. Coaching may not improve motivation but it sure can hinder motivation.

CONTROL

Coaches are always concerned with control. How much control is needed? The answer varies to the team and the coach. A basic rule seems to be that the larger the group the more control is needed. The modern coach is increasingly becoming aware of making the players responsible for their control and discipline. The players must be more responsible for themselves. Some coaches feel that letting the players take responsibility is a loss of their control over the players. Letting the players take responsibility is not giving them free rein to do as they please. Structure is still prevalent and is need more so when control is eased. It is within the structure that the players must be guided. This type of coaching takes extra work and trust in your players.

COMMUNICATIONS

Coaches communicate verbally and nonverbally. It is the nonverbal communications that the coach reveals himself. Nonverbal skills are often called body language. The coach's body language is read by the players. Coaches become unreliable when the players listen to him say one thing while his body language reveals the opposite. Sincerity is the result of body language and verbal language saying the same thing. There is no conflict in the message. Body language is revealed through posture, gestures, facial expressions, mannerisms, etc. Very often the coach does not have to say anything, his body will express it. In verbal communication the way you say it can be more effective than what you say. Things like the pitch and resonance of the voice is critical. The enunciation, speed and rhythm of your talk is also revealing. Of course the loudness of the voice conveys a message.

When giving orders or messages to the players or staff, the coach must make his messages clear, direct, specific and as brief as possible. Leave no room for ambiguity or misinterpretation. If necessary, repeat the message.

ANGER

There will be times that the coach will use anger to express himself and to communicate with the team. At the right time and when necessary anger is justified. It must be remember that anger can be accepted by the players and forgotten with no hard feelings, but, sarcasm and contempt is taken personally and is not forgotten.

A coach who does not employ anger when the players are expecting it and feel they deserve it, may carry the message to the players that the coach does not care. This may not be true, however, the coach is not judged by what he does but by what they think he does.

RULES

Do not have a rule you cannot enforce. If there is something that you want the players to do but you cannot enforce it then it may be best to make it an expectation. A list of team rules should be as brief as possible. Each rule should be relevant and fair. There can be no exceptions to the rules all players will benefit or suffer equally. The players should know what will happen for breaking each rule.

It should be remembered that rules are negative statements and the establishment of rules seems to convey the idea that the players are not able to stay within the expected behavior of the team. When a rule is made it is almost like saying that the player is not capable of expected behavior and must be forced to stay in line.

The use of rules varies from coach to coach and with different levels and ages of the players. The coach and the team should decide on the rules needed to meet the philosophy of the coach, team and players.

GREAT/WEAK COACHES

Weak coaches tell their players what to do. Great coaches build habits and change behavior so that the players know how and are able to do it. Building habits and changing behavior is accomplished through practice sessions with good teaching.

15

DECISION MAKING

Coaching is making decisions. Good coaches make good decisions despite the circumstances. The coach will be hampered or facilitated in his decision making by the following factors:

1. **TIME.** Many times decisions must be made at the moment. Procrastination will not be beneficial. In most cases delaying a decision is worse than the wrong decision. Decisions that drag on create a lack of direction. When a decision is made the players know the course of direction and where they are going. A wrong decision can be corrected if the desired effect is not developing. A wrong decision is not desirable but it is often better than no decision. When coaches are afraid to make a decision the players recognize this hesitancy and lose faith in their leadership. No decisions can also split the group as each player sees the answer differently and each player acts in their own conscious direction. This can soon lead to a lack of unity as each player or clique is off on their own tangent. Decisions made quickly can prevent the team from drawing their own conclusions about what the coach should decide.

2. **INFORMATION.** Decisions must be made with all the possible information available in the time frame. The appropriate time frame can be a few seconds or days. If the decision can be delayed then delay the decision for more facts. Do not delay the decision for fear of making it or hoping the problem will solve itself in a few days. Only delay to gather more information.

3. **ACCEPTANCE.** Acceptance of a decision is best if the group supports the decision. This is not always possible. The players must realize this and sometimes accept the decision for the benefit of the group. Too often players accept decisions on how it affects them personally and not how it is of benefit for the team. Team unity and cohesion helps in the acceptance of decisions.

4. **COACH'S POWER.** The power of the coach is often a factor in the acceptance of decisions. Teams that are winning will tolerate more from the coach because the winning coach has more power and influence. Even though the players may not like the decisions, they will accept the decision because they feel these decisions are helping them to win. Coaches that are losing often have difficulty keeping the players on course as the players feel that they are losing as a result of the coach's decisions.

DECISION MAKING STYLES

The two main style of decision making are autocratic and democratic. Coaches are often labeled as such. Research recognizes that it is often the situation that makes the coach autocratic or democratic and not so much a reflection of his personality. The nature of coaching seems to lead to the autocratic side of the scale.

Autocratic Style

The coach make all the decisions. A subgroup of the autocratic style is the delegating coach, the coach who delegates the decisions to someone or a group. Although the autocratic coach does not make the decision, he is still the one who decides on who is going to make the decision.

Advantages: The players have a consistent pattern of decisions to follow. There are no alternative directions. The players soon know what the coach expects and wants, and they react accordingly. No decisions or input by the players is needed. Many player like this. They just do what they are told. The players have no responsibility to help lead. They have no worries.

Disadvantages: The players have no input. Although some like this, some do not. Players can feel like robots and that they do everything for the coach's glory. They may even feel like slaves responding to the master's commands. Some players may even feel that this is a non-humanistic way of life. When things do not go well then the blame can go directly to the coach.

Democratic Style

The coach and the players share in the decision making process. A subgroup of the democratic style is the consultative coach who consults with one or more players for the decision making process.

Advantages: The players are responsible for their direction. It is their team and their rules. They may feel like leaders or at least like important human beings.

Disadvantages: The democratic process is time consuming as group decisions take time. More team meetings are usually needed. Sometimes a team can be split over a decision with each side not relinquishing to the other. If a compromise is reached, it is often a weak compromise with neither side happy. In situations like this, the players start blaming each other with a "I told you so" attitude when a decision does not meet the demands. Some player feel that they do not want to be told what to do by other players, that the coach should be responsible for decision making. Some players just want to play and make no decisions.

In some decisions, the players do not have the experience or all the information to make the decision. As a result, the chances of a good decision are slim. In cruel terms, a decision by a group of idiots is an idiotic decision. It is well known that decisions by groups are not always effective. The more people making the decision does not mean that the decision will be better. Committees rarely get results on time. Very often the quality of a group decision relies on the best individual in the group. When the best individual makes the decisions the group operates the best.

There is no way one can decide on which style is best. The coach, management, and players will help determine the style needed. It does seem that most players prefer the autocratic style of coaching, especially if it has a humanistic quality. Also, it must be remembered that the greater the pressure of the situation the more the autocratic style is of benefit.

Section 6

Team Strategy

This section is vital to team play. There are many strategies outlined in this section. The coach must select the strategy that will fit his personnel. It would be unwise to select a strategy if the players cannot play to strategy demands. A wise coach will evaluate his players and then determine which strategy will be most effective.

INTRODUCTION TO TEAM STRATEGY

A coach in devising his strategy can adhere to one of the systems outlined, or he can take pieces from each system. He must, however, keep in mind that one stage must flow smoothly into the next stage. A forechecking philosophy must smoothly flow into the backchecking strategy without a scramble for new positions. The backchecking strategy must coordinate with the defensive strategy. The defensive strategy must coordinate with the breakout play. The breakout play must work into the attack and the attack must develop into the forechecking patterns.

Hockey is a fast moving game that switches from offense to defense in split seconds. An attack is of little value if there is an immediate switch of puck possession and the players are out of position for defensive play. It is imperative that strategy flows from one stage to the other. In fact, all strategy flows in a circular pattern as shown in the below diagram.

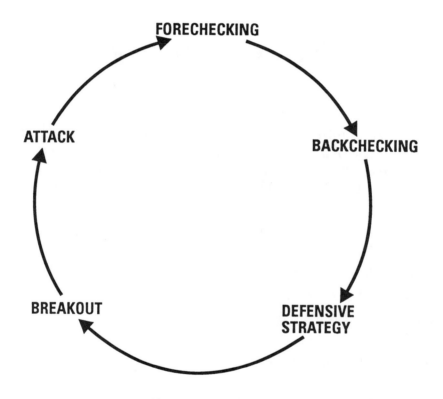

KEY TO DIAGRAMS

⟶ **Skating Direction**

〰⟶ **Backward Skating**

→→→ **Pass or Shot - direction of pass**

◯ **Player**

X **Opposition - no designated player**

(BC) **Backchecker**

(W₁) **Player 1 - usually left-winger**

(W₂) **Player 2 - usually right-winger**

(C) **Player 3 - usually centerman**

(D₄) **Player 4 - usually left defense**

(D₅) **Player 5 - usually right defense**

C **Centerman opposition**

LW **Left Wing**

RW **Right Wing**

LD **Left Defenseman Opposition**

RD **Right Defenseman Opposition**

(G) **Goaltender**

• **Puck**

——⟨ **Check or Pick**

– – – – – **Alternate Route**

16

BASIC TEAM STRATEGIES

Hockey strategy breaks down into two basic situations — the 1 on 1 and the 2 on 1. Offensive team strategy usually is geared to developing a 2 on 1 situation to gain advantage for puck possession or for a scoring opportunity. Defensive strategy is geared to prevent this 2 on 1 development by countering with the 1 on 1 against each offensive threat.

All situations are an extension of the 1 on 1 and the 2 on 1. The 3 on 2, 3 on 1, 2 on 2, and the rest are simply multiples of the 2 on 1 and 1 on 1. For instance, the 2 on 2 is a 1 on 1 with each man. The 3 on 2 is a 2 on 1 with one defender and a 1 on 1 with the other defender, or it can be a 2 on 1 with each defender.

In utilizing or countering these situations, a team should have a consistent philosophy of execution. If each player knows his responsibility during a given situation, he will be able to react in an organized manner without the confusion or duplication of duties.

The basic team strategies will be discussed offensively and defensively and their application applies to all strategies in this book.

BASIC TEAM STRATEGIES - DEFENSIVE

Defensive strategy is based on playing the percentages. This means it is better to force the opposition to shoot from well out rather than from close in. There is a greater percentage in stopping the long shots than the close ones. Playing the percentages also means to force the shots on goal from an angle rather than from the slot (the central position in front of the goal net). Defensively, a team tries to keep the opposition from controlling the puck in the slot because of the high percentage of scoring possibilities in this area.

Playing the percentages is particularly evident where the opposition has the man advantage as in the 2 on 1 or 3 on 2 situations. This happens quite frequently as the opposition, when on the attack, will try to gain a man advantage to the situation. Since a defender cannot be in two places at once, the coverage must be geared to the most dangerous man or the man with the greater percentage of scoring.

In defensive situations, and even in the offensive strategy, the goaltender must be involved in the strategy. Too many times the goaltender is simply left to play the shot from wherever it comes. If the goaltender knows what his teammates are doing, then he can react quickly by anticipating the possible play. If the goaltender and the defensemen coordinate their efforts, they have an excellent chance of neutralizing the attack. If a backchecker enters into the defensive strategy, he must also have definite responsibilities so that the whole team knows what is happening and what will happen.

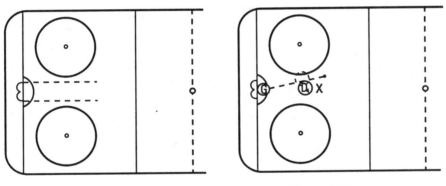

Figure 16-1   Figure 16-2

The defensemen, in playing their attacker(s), should use an imaginary guide line as their back up line (figure 16-1). This back up line is just off the goal post and along the slot area's edge. Further diagrams will show how these guide lines come into play.

ONE ON ONE - Defensive

The defenseman (figure 16-2) must play the body and not the puck. His main purpose is to force the attacker to the side and out of the slot or to force the shot well out from the goal net. The defenseman must not lunge at his check or any similar type of action that would give the attacker clear access to the goal in the event he misses his check. This type of play may be possible if a backchecker is in good position to cover.

A backchecker on the 1 on 1 plays the puck, unless the goalie clears the puck. The backchecker must be alert because the goalie can clear the puck to the backchecker for a quick break out of the end zone.

By playing the puck carrier's body, the defenseman leaves the goalie with a sight line (clear line of vision) to the puck. If the defenseman is playing the puck, he will often be positioned in front of the puck and thus help screen the puck from the goalie. In figure 16-2, the defenseman is playing the body and leaves the goalie with a sight line to the puck. The dotted circle represents the defenseman when playing the puck and blocking the goalie's vision of the puck.

If the puck carrier approaches down the center ice area (figure 16-3), the defenseman must force the attacker to the side and out of the slot area so that a possible shot by the attacker will be from a poor angle.

The defenseman must always play the man after the shot so that the goalie or backchecker has time to clear or control the puck. The defenseman must not let the attacker slip past him for a second chance on goal or to regain puck possession.

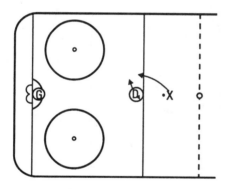

Figure 16-3

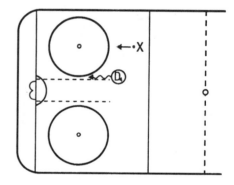

Figure 16-4

If the puck carrier approaches from the side (figure 16-4), the defenseman should follow his imaginary guide line back to the goal to prevent his check from cutting into the slot area. The defenseman simply keeps the attacker to the outside so that his shot will be from a poor angle. If the defenseman moves to close to the boards and plays his attacker head on, then it is easier for the attacker to cut into the slot for a quick shot on goal. Another advantage in staying on the guide line is that if another attacker moves into the attack for a 2 on 1 situation, the defenseman is in position for the extra attacker.

If the attacker is alone and the defenseman has a very strong possibility of stopping the attacker early by moving closer to the boards then such a risk may be worthy. Remember, there must be a very strong possibility.

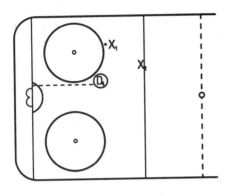

Figure 16-5

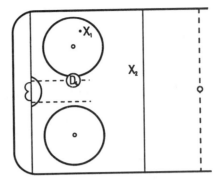

Figure 16-6

TWO ON ONE - Defensive

Basically, the goalie has the puck carrier and the defenseman has the other man (figure 16-5). The defenseman remains on his back up line and plays for the possible pass by X1 to X2. He also tries to force the puck carrier into shooting from a poor angle.

The defenseman must back up even with the puck carrier so that the puck carrier is unable to cut in behind him to the goal (figure 16-6).

If the puck carrier X1 does cut for the front of the goal net, then the defenseman D must play him while the goalie is now prepared for the possible shot from the slot by X2. The backchecker picks up the slot man X2.

The defenseman D cannot play both men, so he must play the percentages by keeping X2 well out of the slot and yet keep X1 from cutting in behind him into the slot area close to the goal. If X1 does pass to X2 as he is making his cut to the goal, then the goaltender has time to move out of the goal to cut the angle of the shot on goal. If the goaltender does not know what his defenseman D is going to do, or who he covers, then the goalie must play both forwards, and, as a result, he cannot move out of the goal because he does not know if D will stop X1. This makes the goalie's reaction to a slot shot by X2 to be hesitant or late.

The defenseman (figure 16-7) should not try to cover both forwards. If he tries to go to both forwards (puck chasing) he ends up covering no one and the goalie is left with confusion in trying to stop both attackers.

Frequently, the defenseman rushes out at the slot man and the slot man gets the puck away before the defenseman gets to him. This places the defenseman between the two attackers and covering neither one. This rush by the defenseman often results in a good screen on his goaltender, while the attacking wing X1 positions himself in front of the goal for a tip-in, screen or rebound.

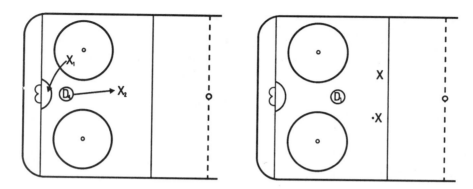

Figure 16-7   *Figure 16-8*

If both attackers are coming down the middle (figure 16-8), the strategy is much the same. The defenseman stays in the slot area leaving the area outside the slot open for the shot. This again is playing the percentages of having the opposition shoot from a bad angle.

THREE ON ONE - Defensive

The defenseman (figure 16-9) plays the slot area and tries to force the puck to the side for a poor angle shot. If the puck is to the side, the defenseman uses his backup line as in the 2 on 1. The defenseman must try to position himself on the back up line so as to cut off a pass to the far wing X3. Such a pass forces the goalie into a long move to the other side of the goal. If the puck carrier X1 was forced to pass to the slot man X2 the goalie would have a short move with more time to move out and cut the angle.

If a backchecker is present, he should take X3 as he is deep in the slot area with an open net facing him. X3 has a higher percentage of scoring as he is deep in the slot while X2 is well out from the goal.

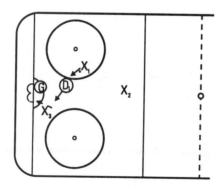
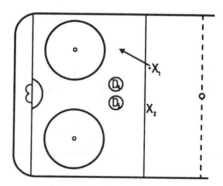

Figure 16-9   *Figure 16-10*

TWO ON TWO - Defensive

The 2 on 2 can be a 1 on 1 with each defenseman (figure 16-10). The near defenseman D4 forces the puck carrier to the side and out of the slot area. The other defenseman D5 covers his man X2 and also watches for a possible pass play.

The backchecker plays the slot area for a rebound, pass or to pick up a late attacker.

If both attackers X1 and X2 shift to the side (figure 16-11) to set up a 2 on 1 with D4, then D5 shifts over to cover his check X2.

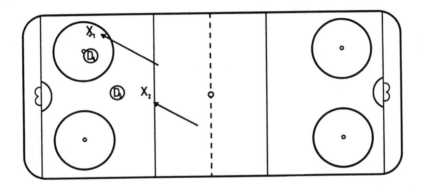

Figure 16-11

If a backchecker is present he takes X2 while D5 moves to his slot coverage in front of the goal

Very often in a 2 on 2 the defenseman can be more aggressive and attack the attackers (fiqure 16-12).

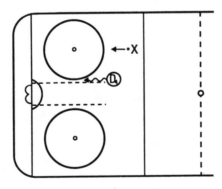

Figure 16-12

The far defenseman D5 moves forward to angle the puck carrier X1 to the boards. D5 plays the body and is often very capable of giving a good body check. D4 can pick up the puck on this play.

Note the positioning of the two defensemen D4 and D5 (figure 16-12). They are inside their checks and not facing them even up. The defensemen are on their back up line. By being inside their checks they are helping to force the play to the side.

The backchecker moves into the slot area and picks up the puck or winger depending on the situation.

ONE ON TWO - Defensive

This is an aggressive or forcing situation (figure 16-13) and is played like the previous 2 on 2 situation. One defenseman D5 plays the puck carrier's body, body checks him, while the other defenseman D4 plays the puck.

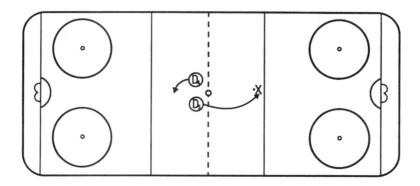

Figure 16-13

In the 1 on 2 situation (figure 16-14), the defensemen should move towards a tandem position rather than a parallel system.

Diagram A shows a parallel system and what happens when one defenseman is beat by the puck carrier who skates around him. Notice how D5 must chase the puck carrier as their is no backup strategy.

Diagram B shows the tandem position of the defensemen. D5 is the back up to the play and is in position to play the puck carrier is the puck carrier moves around the first defenseman D4.

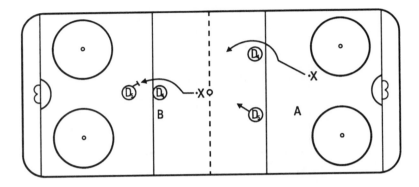

Figure 16-14

THREE ON TWO - Defensive

When the puck carrier is in the middle (figure 16-15), the defensemen maintain their back up line and force the shot or pass from well out or from the poor angle.

If the wing has the puck (figure 16-16) the near defenseman D4 plays him as a 2 on 1 situation with the emphasis on the puck carrier X1. The far defenseman D5 also plays a 2 on 1 with X2 and X3 with the emphasis on X3. As explained under the 3 on 1, if the far wing X3 is left open he usually has an open net to shoot at because the goalie has the long move to the far goal post.

The backchecker plays the slot man X2.

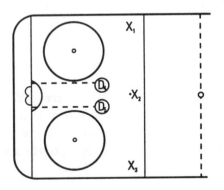

Figure 16-15

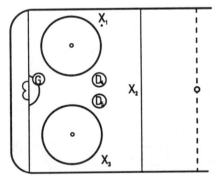

Figure 16-16

One of the most common problems in defending against the 3 on 2 is that the far defenseman (figure 16-17) tries to cover two men at the same time and thus cover no one.

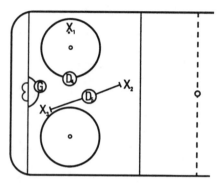

Figure 16-17   *Figure 16-18*

D5 is trying to cover X3 and X2 at the same time, and, as a result, he is ineffective against both attackers. It must be remembered that one cannot be in two places at the same time. D5 should cover X3 who has the open net to shoot at if he gets the puck. X3 can also be an effective screen to the goaltender as well as in position for a tip-in or rebound. X2 is the goaltender's man. If X2 does get the puck, the goalie has time to move out to cut the angle on a shot by X2. As previously mentioned, if X3 gets the puck, the goalie has a long move to the far post and little chance of stopping the quick shot by X3.

BASIC TEAM STRATEGIES - OFFENSIVE

ONE ON ZERO - Offensive

This is a break-a-way on the goaltender (figure 16-18). Perhaps the main strategy is not to panic and rush the attempt on goal. The attacker must remain cool and make the goaltender commit himself by making the first move.

TWO ON ZERO - Offensive

This is a two man break-a-way (figure 16-19). Usually, the puck carrier W1 draws the goaltender to one side of the goal net and uses a quick pass to this teammate W2 who has the open net for a shot on goal. As sometimes happens and to prevent unsuccessful attempts, the attackers must not become too fancy or complicated in their strategy.

ONE ON ONE - Offensive

It is very difficult to beat or get around a good defenseman on a 1 on 1 situation (figure 16-20). Often the best strategy is to use the fake shot and dekes to move the defenseman into position so that he can be used as a screen for a shot on goal.

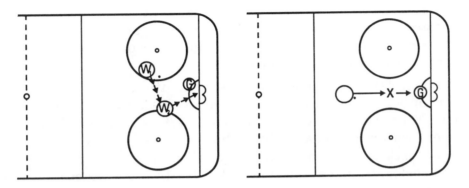

Figure 16-19   *Figure 16-20*

The puck carrier must maintain his slot position and not let himself be forced out of the slot area unless he plans to drift to give a teammates time to get into position for a 2 on 1 situation.

TWO ON ONE - Offensive

The winger (figure 16-21) carries the puck in wide and deep and then breaks for the goal net. The centerman maintains the slot but hangs back. If the puck carrier W1 cannot make it to the goal, ha passes back to C3.

W1 tries to draw X toward him to help open up the slot area for C3.

If W1 passes to C3, then he must continue to the goal mouth for a screen, tip-in, pass, or rebound.

If the play is down the middle (figure 16-22), the same basic strategy is employed. The puck carrier W1 drifts to the side to pull the defenseman with him to open up the area for his teammate W2. Once the defenseman X leaves W2 open, W1 passes back to W2 in the slot.

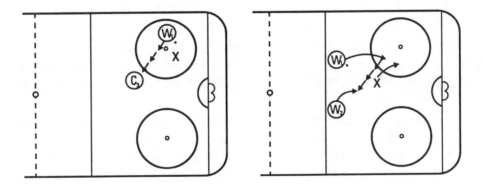

Figure 16-21   *Figure 16-22*

In this strategy down the middle, the puck carrier plays the role of the winger (breaks wide) and the non-puck carrier becomes the centerman (high in the slot) and slows down for the pass back play.

A variation of the 2 on 1 play is the crisscross pattern (figure 16-23). This pattern can be complicated but it can be effective if it is executed in a precise manner. The puck carrier crosses in front of his teammate and draws the defender X with him. Once X is going with W1 and the slot is opened up, then W1 passes back (or across) to W2. It is important for W1 to wait until X moves with him before he makes the pass back play. If W1 passes too soon, the defender has a chance to redirect his movement to prevent the pass back. Timing is crucial to this play. Faulty execution of the crisscross just creates confusion among the team and no deception to the defender.

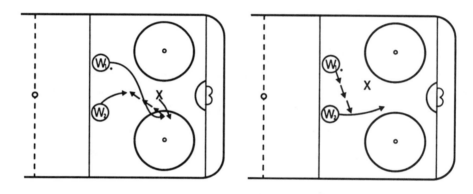

Figure 16-23   Figure 16-24

If the defenseman X is lined up straight on the puck carrier W1 (figure 16-24), the non-puck carrier breaks for the goal and receives a pass from the puck carrier W1.

The puck carrier W1 hangs back for a possible return pass in the event the defender X is able to move over and cover W2.

A common mistake on the 2 on 1 is for the two attackers to move too close together (figure 16-25). This closeness makes it easier for the defender X to cover both attackers. Also, C3 is not in the slot and has a poor angle shot if he does get the puck.

Another common mistake is a lack of triangulation by the attackers (figure 16-26). W1 and W2 form a straight line with the defender X. This means that the puck carrier must pass through X to pass the puck to his teammate W2. Notice how W2 would be open for a pass if he positioned himself as in the dotted line of triangulation.

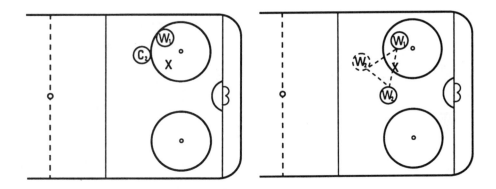

Figure 16-25   *Figure 16-26*

THREE ON ONE - Offensive

The strategy (figure 16-27) is to get the puck to the W1 to pull the defenseman over. The goalie also has to move to cover W1 for a possible shot on goal. W2 is the far winger and he positions himself off the far goal post so that a quick pass to him will give him an open net to shoot at. Such a pass play forces the goaltender into a difficult and extremely fast move to the far goal post.

W1 and C3 play the 2 on 1 situation on the puck side to help open up the slot area for W2. Note the triangulation of the three attackers. This gives the puck carrier W1 an alternative if he cannot get the puck to his far winger W2.

TWO ON TWO - Offensive

The attackers (figure 16-28) can shift to the side, if they are not already to the side, to set up the 2 on 1 with one of the defensemen. If the attackers stay in the middle, they will have to contend with a 1 on 1 situation with each attacker. Any of the 2 on 1 plays can be utilized.

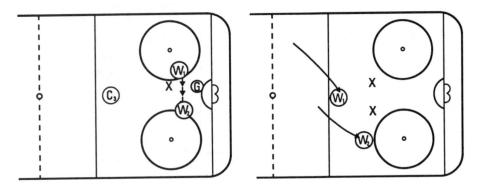

Figure 16-27   *Figure 16-28*

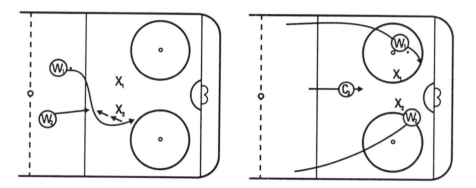

Figure 16-29   *Figure 16-30*

Sometimes, the 2 on 1 crisscross can be effective if the attackers are coming down the center ice area (figure 16-29). The puck carrier W1 cuts over in front of W2 and pulls X2 with him. Once X2 is moving with W1, W1 passes to W2.

THREE ON TWO - Offensive

The wing W1 (figure 16-30) carries the puck over the blue line and sets up the 2 on 1 with his centerman against the near defenseman X1. The far winger breaks for the goal net.

If a backchecker is on the centerman during the 3 on 2 rush (figure 16-31) then the centerman breaks for the goal net while the far wing cuts over to take the slot position. The far winger is the key to this play. As the attack progresses, the far wing must look and read the play. If he sees his centerman breaking for the goal net because of a backchecker, then he must cut over to the slot position.

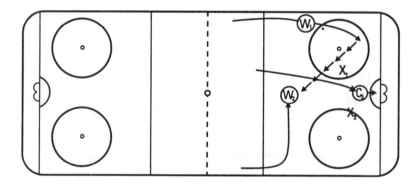

Figure 16-31

This strategy helps to shake loose a backchecker or pull the backchecker towards the goal net so as to open up the slot area for the far wing man. The three attackers still maintain good triangulation and positional play with a man C3 in front of the goal and a man W2 high in the slot for a shot or for backchecking.

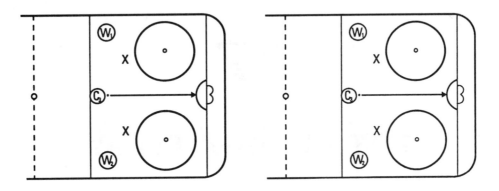

Figure 16-31   *Figure 16-32*

If the defensemen are playing too wide (figure 16-32), the centerman C3 may have an opening straight to the goal net.

If the defensemen are high and close together and not moving back too fast (figure 16-33), then fast breaking wingers can break around the defense and take a soft pass from the centerman or play the centers shot on goal.

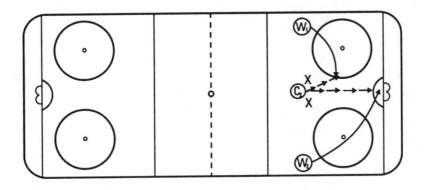

Figure 16-33

17

THE BREAKOUT PLAY

This may well be the most important play in hockey. A hockey team must be able to breakout of its own end in order to go on the attack. Naturally, if a team cannot breakout of its own end zone, it will be in trouble. This breakout play will work with the various strategies in this book. Other breakout plays are covered in the strategy section.

THE BREAKOUT PLAY FROM BEHIND THE GOAL NET

Once positive puck possession is gained in the defensive end zone, the players move to their breakout positions. Very often puck possession is gained behind the goal net or the puck is passed behind the net to organize the breakout play. The breakout play must be simple and yet have variety and diversity to give difficulty to the opposition. The players must have alternative plays if their first play choice is blocked. The alternative plays should be in a systematic order so that each player knows what is happening and what is to happen next. The systematic order of the players knowing the strategy enables the team to think as a unit.

The key to the breakout play is positive puck possession. The players must not move to their breakout positions until the team has positive control of the puck. If the players move to their breakout positions when puck possession is uncertain, they may be leaving their checks open for a quick scoring chance if the opposition gets puck control.

A good breakout play will move the puck out quickly and trap some of the opposing team's forecheckers deep in the end zone. Trapping puts the forecheckers in position to be late in their backchecking duties. To trap the forecheckers, the breakout players must position themselves to breakout quickly, and yet they must also be in position to protect defensively if puck possession is lost. If the forwards are deep in the end zone, they can provide protection if the puck possession is lost and are also in position for a quick pass. By being too deep in the end zone, the players may have difficulty in breaking out as well as trapping the opposition deep in the end zone.

If the forwards are placed well up to the blue line, they can breakout quickly, although they may offer less protection defensively. Passing to forwards on the blue line is difficult and can be dangerous. However, it can also be very effective.

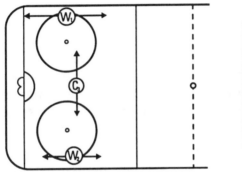
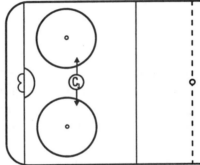

Figure 17-1   Figure 17-2

The positioning of W1, W2 and C3 (figure 17-1) will depends on the situation and the opposition. Sometimes they will have to move in deep and sometimes they will have to stay out near the blue line. Although they have a choice of positioning, they should stay in their basic positioning. Notice how on the breakout play the wings move wide to the boards. This opens up the attack and gives the defensive team more area to cover.

The players must not breakout before the puck carrier is ready. Wingers that break too soon will kill the attack from the defensive zone. A good rule to follow is to wait for the puck carrier to lift his head and show readiness. From this "key" the players can react.

The first choice on the breakout is to pass to the centerman in the mid-ice area. The centerman should skate back and forth (figure 17-2), parallel to the blue line, for a pass. He must be careful if skating vertically to the blue line as he will have to receive a pass while looking over his shoulder. Besides being dangerous to take a pass this way, it is difficult to pass accurately under such conditions.

If the centerman is outside the blue line (figure 17-3), he should cross the blue line to the side so that he can break parallel to the blue line to receive the pass.

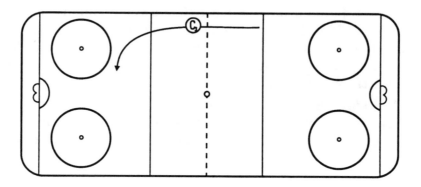

Figure 17-3

If the mid-ice area is too congested (figure 17-4) then the centerman will go behind the goal net to help organize the breakout. He should proceed at about half to three quarter speed. While going behind the goal net, the centerman must look to the area around the goal net for opposition forecheckers so he can decide on one of two alternatives: taking the puck or leaving the puck with the defenseman.

If the centerman takes the puck because it is clear of forecheckers in front of the goal, he should immediately cut up the middle between his wingers.

The centerman (figure 17-5) takes the puck and finds that he is blocked by a forechecker immediately, he simply drops the puck back to the defenseman who is trailing the centerman or, if possible, he makes a quick pass to the wing.

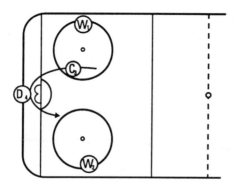

Figure 17-4

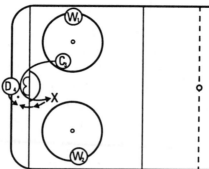

Figure 17-5

If the centerman (figure 17-6) leaves the puck for the defenseman because the center ice lane is blocked by a forechecker, he will proceed wide to the corner and the winger on his side will break into the center area to become the centerman. The winger must break straight across and parallel to the blue line. The defenseman can pass to the centerman C3 or to the breaking winger W2. It is possible that the defenseman may even move the puck to the other side to pass to the far winger who may be open.

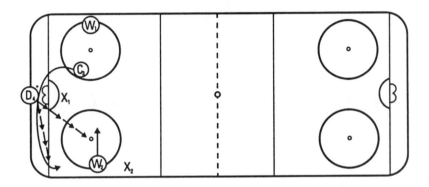

Figure 17-6

This same play can be used by the winger to leave his check on the boards. If the forechecker X2 moves with W2 then C3 has clear access out of the end zone and D4 can give him the pass.

Simplified, the rules are as follows:

1. Do not break too soon. Wait until everything is ready.

2. Pass to the centerman in the mid-ice area.

3. If the centerman has to go behind the goal net, he will either take the puck or leave the puck with the defenseman.

4. If the centerman takes the puck, he breaks up the middle. If the centerman leaves the puck, he goes wide to the corner while the winger breaks to the center.

This breakout play has a consistency and a sequence of player movement. The diversity and variety result in the options of where to move the puck.

18

THE THREE-TWO SYSTEM

The three-two system is the most often employed by present day hockey teams in North America. Its name is derived from the formation of three forwards and two defensemen. Although this formation may alter in the defensive and offensive end zones, the basic strategy is to have the three forwards working as one unit while the two defensemen play as another. This system can be effective despite the change in checks in each end zone. The change in checks is the result of the winger covering the opposition's winger, but he often ends up covering the defenseman in the end zones. Unfortunately, the switching from winger coverage to defenseman coverage can create problems. The three-two system has a strong zone coverage with some man-to-man coverage.

DEFENSIVE END ZONE PLAY

The end zone coverage has several patterns. They are:

1. Winger in puck corner and the centerman on the point (opposing defenseman).
2. Both wings on the points.
3. First forward in the corner, second forward on the point.
4. One man covering both points.

The following diagrams will clarify these patterns.

156

Winger in Puck Corner and Center On Near Point

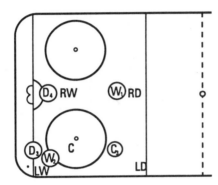
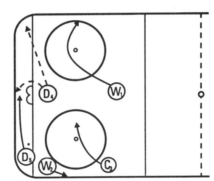

Figure 18-1   *Figure 18-2*

The near winger W2 (figure 18-1) goes into the corner to help the defenseman D5 gain puck possession. The centerman C3 remains back to cover the point LD. The far winger W1 is high in the slot covering the point RD and helping the defenseman D4 with slot coverage. The strategy between the near defenseman and the near winger in gaining puck possession is for the first player to play the man and the second player to get the puck.

Once puck possession is gained (figure 18-2), the players move to their breakout positions. The wings move to the boards while the centerman C3 loops into the center area for the breakout pass. The defenseman D4 remains in front of the goal net if he is in doubt or feels it is not safe to leave the slot area. D4 must not leave the slot area unless a teammate has positive puck possession. When it is safe, D4 can go behind the goal or into the far corner to receive a pass from D5. One advantage of this end zone formation is that the wings are at the boards and the center is in the center ice area for the breakout. The centerman plays close to the boards so that he can play the puck if it is banged up the boards and also so he has a good angle to loop into the center ice for the breakout.

For the breakout (figure 18-3), D5 can pass to D4, W1, W2, and C3 if he is able to gain possession behind the goal net. If he is not able to get behind the goal net, then he can make his breakout pass before he gets behind the net. Quite often, if he is alert, D4 can take the pass by skating into the corner.

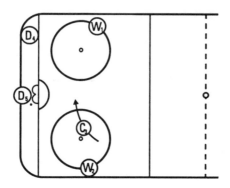

Figure 18-3

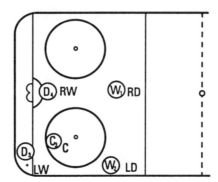

Figure 18-4

Both Wings on the Point

This strategy (figure 18-4) is similar to the previous one, except the centerman C3 goes into the corner to help the defenseman gain puck possession. Notice how in most cases C3 will position himself a little more to the net while backing up his defenseman D5. The same corner play strategy applies in that the defenseman plays the man and the centerman picks up the puck. When puck possession is gained, the breakout play is executed. An advantage of this system is in the simplicity of execution — wingers on the points and centerman in the corners. Each has a clearly defined role to play.

First Forward in the Corner, Second Forward on the Point

The player who gets to the puck the fastest (the first forward), between the winger and the centerman (figure 18-5), goes in to help the defenseman while the other player (the second forward) covers the point. The far winger W1 goes into the slot area. The breakout applies once puck possession is gained.

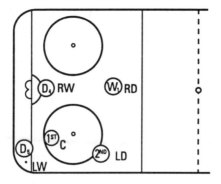

Figure 18-5

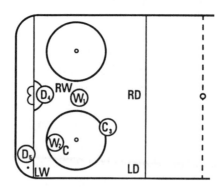

Figure 18-6

One Man Covering Both Points

The centerman C3 (figure 18-6) covers both points. This strategy gives weak point coverage but strong coverage low in the slot, around the goal mouth, and in the puck corner. This may be dangerous if the opposition has strong point play. When puck possession is gained, then the players move to the breakout play.

OFFENSIVE END ZONE PLAY

Offensive end zone play is based on triangulation of the three forwards. The three systems are:

1. Winger in the corner

2. Center in the corner

3. First in the corner, second backup

Winger in the Corner

The winger W1 (figure 18-7), plays the corner with the centerman C3 backing him up. The winger W1 plays the man while the centerman C3 picks up the puck. The far winger W2 plays the slot. The positioning of C3 will vary according to the opposition. C3 can play tight to W1 to give two men on the puck (position 1) or he can play a little more back (position 2) to give only one man on the puck. C3 in the second position (2) gives extra backchecking potential as well as position to attack the corner or the goal net.

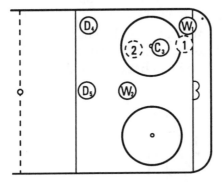
Figure 18-7

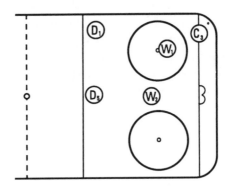
Figure 18-8

Centerman in the Corner

The centerman C3 in the corner (figure 18-8) utilizes the same strategy as previously outlined. An advantage of this system is that the two wingers W1 and W2 are in position for backchecking duties.

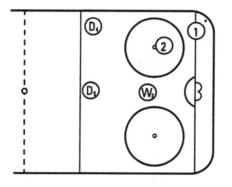 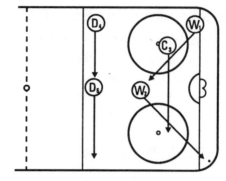

Figure 18-9   Figure 18-10

First in the Corner, Second Backup

Once again the strategy is the same (figure 18-9) except that the player who can get to the puck first (1) goes into the corner and the second player (2) plays back up. The far winger covers the slot.

Player Movement When the Puck Moves to Other Corner

When the puck moves quickly to the other corner (figure 18-10) the following rotation occurs. The slotman W2 goes to the puck corner while the backup man C3 moves over to back up W2. The far winger W1 moves to the slot position. This rotation leaves the wings to their own side of the ice. The defensemen simply shifts with the puck.

If the centerman C3 is in the corner (figure 18-11) and the coach does not desire to have his wing move over to the other side of the ice to back up the corner, he can use this pattern. The wing W1 moves to the slot position, while the centerman C3 cuts across to take his backup with W2. The weakness in this system is that it takes a little longer for C3 to be in back up position. The defensemen shift with the puck.

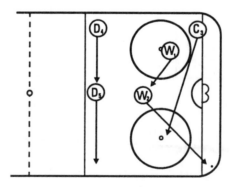

Figure 18-11

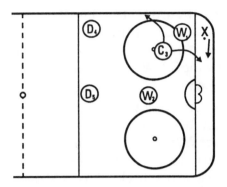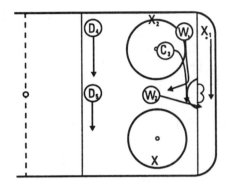

Figure 18-12   Figure 18-13

If the opposition X gains puck possession (figure 18-12) and escapes from W1, then the backup man C3 moves in to play the puck carrier. The defensemen D4 and D5 must be alert for the quick breakout pass by the opposition.

If the puck is carried behind the goal net by the opposition X1, then the players use this strategy (figure 18-13). W1 chases the puck carrier and forces him to go behind the goal net. C3 angles the puck carrier to go behind the goal net. If C3 can stop the puck carrier before he gets behind the goal net then C3 should do so; otherwise, C3 continues in front of the goal net to be backup man on the other side. W2 cuts in off the goal net to pick up the puck carrier. W2 must time his move precisely with the puck carrier. If W2 moves too slow then the puck carrier will skate by W2 and if W2 moves too fast then the puck carrier will cut behind W2 and break out. The defensemen D4 and D5 shift with the play. If the puck carrier X1 stops behind the goal net, then the following two plays (figure 18-14 and figure 18-15) will be effective.

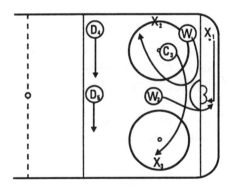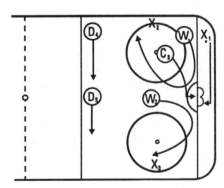

Figure 18-14   Figure 18-15

If the puck carrier X1 stops behind the goal (figure 18-14), then W2 can go behind the goal net to play puck carrier X1 while C3 continues to the boards to cover the opposition's wing. When C3 sees W2 definitely going behind the goal net then that is his key to cover the far wing X3. W1 loops around to pick up his check X2. The defense shift with the play.

If W2 is unable to play the puck carrier X1 effectively behind the goal net (figure 18-15), W2 can leave the puck carrier for C3 who stops in front of the net to play the puck carrier X1. If C3 sees that W2 does not go behind the goal net, then C3 must remain in front of the goal net to play the puck carrier X1. W2 continues his pattern to the boards to pick up his check X3. W1 also loops around to pick his check X2. The defense shifts with the play.

With this offensive end zone strategy the wings can break off for backchecking duties, or as in figure 18-16, the backup man C3 and the far winger W2 can peel off for backchecking duties.

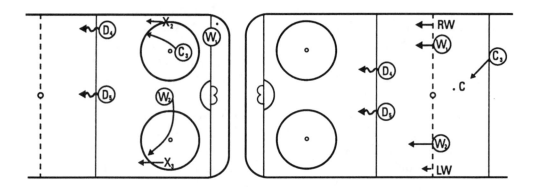

Figure 18-16   *Figure 18-17*

In choosing a pattern for defensive end zone play (figure 18-17), the strategy must coordinate with the offensive end zone play so that backchecking duties do not cause confusion in the defensive end zone. Confusion of backchecking duties may occur when the wing and center switch duties while forechecking. When the backchecking moves into the defensive end zone there may be confusion as to when the wing and center will return to their respective positions.

FACE-OFF POSITIONS

Defensive End Zone Face-off

Figure 18-18 is the standard face-off formation. W1 covers RD. W2 covers LW wherever LW is positioned. D4 is on the face-off circle to cover RW and while remaining in the slot area. If C3 gets the draw to D5, D5 goes behind the goal net to set up the breakout play. If the situation presents itself, D5 can break up the boards towards LD. In most cases, LD will back out of the end zone if the play comes toward him. If D5 cannot get by LD, he can pass the puck off the boards into the neutral ice area.

Offensive End Zone Face-off

Figure 18-19 is the standard face-off formation. Variations of this standard formation and the face-off formation for the pulled goalie are covered in Chapter 19: "The Box Strategies."

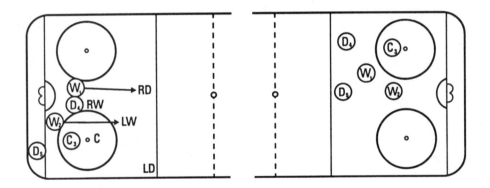

Figure 18-18   Figure 18-19

PENALTY KILLING - THE BOX FORMATION

Defensive End Zone - One Man Short

The Box (figure 18-20) is the standard penalty killing formation. The main purpose of this strategy is to keep the puck to the outside and away from the slot area.

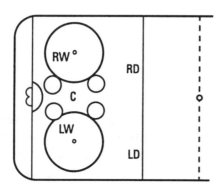

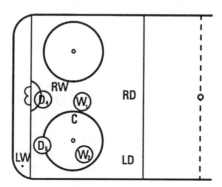

Figure 18-20   Figure 18-21

When the puck is in the corner (figure 18-21), the near defenseman D5 moves out but does not attack the puck unless he is able to gain positive possession. The main strategy of D5 is to keep LW in the corner or force him to pass. D5 must not let LW get by him and into the slot area. The opposition's slot man C is covered by W1. W1 is the farthest man from the puck.

If the opposition's pointman LD has the puck (figure 18-22), he is covered by W2 who must remain between LD and the goal. The slotman C is covered by W1.

If LD passes to RD (figure 18-23), then W1 moves out to cover RD and W2 moves into the slot on C. D5 adjusts accordingly.

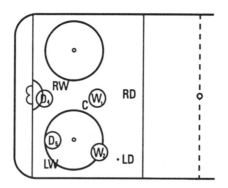

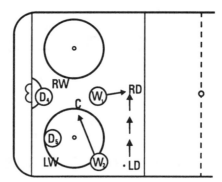

Figure 18-22   Figure 18-23

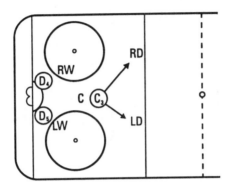

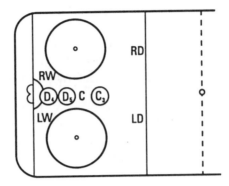

Figure 18-24   Figure 18-25

Defensive End Zone - Two Men Short

Figure 18-24 is the basic triangle system. C3 covers both points while the defense is responsible for the goal net area. This system is losing favor with many coaches for the rotating system explained in Chapter 19 - "The Box Strategies."

Another system for the two men short situation is the tandem formation (figure 18-25). This formation covers the slot and forces the shots from a poor angle. The three defenders are in a straight line to give strong slot coverage, especially against C. C3 covers both points while D4 and D5 shift as necessary to the two most dangerous men between RW, C, and LW.

Forechecking - One Man Short

W1 (figure 18-26), the first forechecker, forechecks and peels off to one wing. W2, the backup to W1, goes to the side opposite W1. Each will pick up a wing to backcheck.

Another forechecking strategy (figure 18-27) is to have the forwards W1 and W2 go to the opposition's wings and leave the center ice lane open. Backchecking begins from this positioning. The reasoning for this strategy is that rarely is a forechecker able to do much damage against a power play breakout so why not let the opposition get started. By moving immediately to cover their respective players, there is less chance of a forechecker getting caught or trapped in the end zone. When a forechecker is trapped in the end zone the opposition is breaking out against only three defenders.

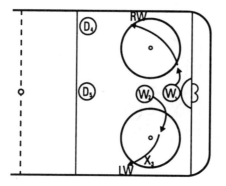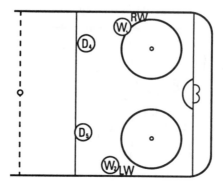

Figure 18-26   Figure 18-27

Backchecking - One Man Short

The backcheckers (figure 18-28) are needed so that the defensemen D4 and D5 can "stand-up" in front of the blue line to force the attack at the blue line. When the four defenders are able to force the play at the blue line the opposition has difficulty against the wall of defenders.

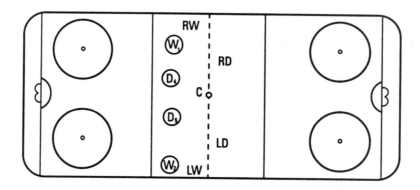

Figure 18-28

THE POWER PLAY

Defensive End Zone Power Play

In most cases, the breakout will originate behind the goal net (figure 18-29). The breakout play as outlined in Chapter 16 can be used effectively. In most cases, defenseman D5 (in front of the goal net) moves out to the wing W2 and skates with the wing up the ice but slightly behind the wing. By staying slightly behind the wing, the puck carrier is able to pass to the wing or the breaking defenseman D5. With the defenseman breaking with the winger, the attack has a strong side for advantage in penetration to the opposition's goal. The defenseman D4, behind the goal net, trails the play as the back up. If desired, it is possible to have D4 breakup the side opposite to the other defenseman D5 for two strong sides to the attack.

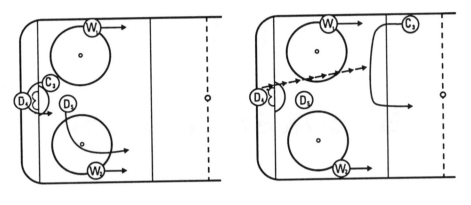

Figure 18-29   Figure 18-30

An effective and quick breakout (figure 18-30) is to sometimes have the centerman C3 delay his return to his defensive end zone so that he can cut parallel to the blue line and receive a long pass from D4. This play is extremely effective in trapping an opposition's forechecker deep in the end zone.

Offensive End Zone - Power Play

Figure 18-31 is the standard power play formation. Various patterns can be developed by passing the puck to set up 2 on 1 situations and by shifting C3 to various corners of the box and slot area. There are many power play strategies and they are discussed in detail in Chapter 19 - "The Box Strategies."

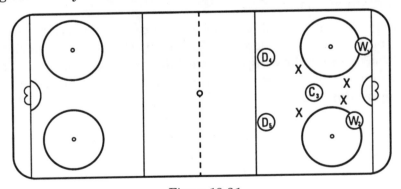

Figure 18-31

19

THE BOX STRATEGIES

As the name implies, the players play a box pattern with an extra man. The various box patterns are the 2-1-2, 1-2-2, 3-2 box, and the 2-3 box. The 2-1-2 is the main strategy while the other patterns are simply variations of the 2-1-2. For this reason, the 2-1-2 is explained in more detail than the other strategies. Techniques from the 2-1-2 will apply to the other box strategies.

THE 2-1-2 STRATEGY

The 2-1-2 system, also known as the five man box, is a unique system that breaks from the traditional concepts and strategies. In analyzing the wingers' checking responsibilities, one will note that when the winger is attacking or forechecking, he is continually confronted with the opposition's defenseman. This is clearly evident in the corners, in the slot, on the 2 on 1, on the 2 on 2, and the 3 on 2 situations.

In the wingers' defensive end zone, most systems have the wings covering the points (opposition's defensemen). If a winger is to check and backcheck the opposition's winger, the wing will have difficulty in determining when to leave the wing to cover the defenseman or point. This switching of coverage is confusing and dangerous.

For effective coverage (figure 19-1), the winger takes the opposition's near defenseman (e.g. W1 checks RD). The defensemen will in turn check the opposition near the winger (e.g. D4 checks RW). The centerman covers the opposition centerman. Basketball, soccer, and box lacrosse have proven that this checking system is most effective.

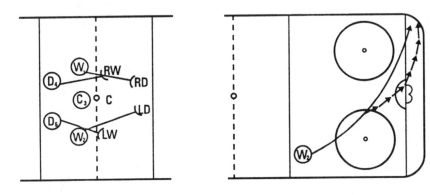

Figure 19-1   *Figure 19-2*

In the 2-1-2 system, the wingers are allowed to roam from side to side of the ice. A winger W1 (figure 19-2) breaking for the goal net can continue into the far corner to chase the puck or make a play. Conventional systems have the winger stop in front of the goal net so that he does not leave his side of the ice. In the 2-1-2 system winger W1 is free to continue his natural momentum into the opposite corner with an excellent chance to be first on the puck.

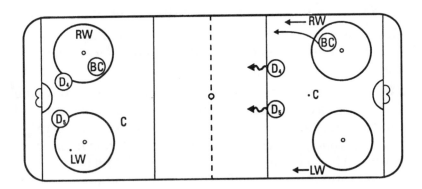

Figure 19-3

When a three man rush (figure 19-3) progresses down the ice against two defensemen (3 on 2), the traditional strategy is to backcheck a wing. The opposition attackers simply pass to the open wing LW and the centerman C works the two-on-one with the one defenseman D5. The other or far defenseman D4 is checking the wing RW and the centerman C. Unfortunately, D4 is often taken out of position to move out to cover the centerman C.

The logical solution to this problem is to have the backchecker cover the centerman C (figure 19-4). When the backchecker BC covers the man in the center C, each defender will have a one-on-one situation: BC checks C, D4 has RW and D5 has LW. The backchecker BC can force the pass by C to a wing and still be in position to cover the slot man in the defensive end zone.

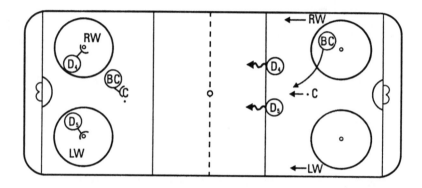

Figure 19-4

In executing the 2-1-2 system (figure 19-5), the key is the role of the centerman who positions himself to form triangulation with his defensemen in the offensive end zone, the neutral ice zone and the defensive end zone. Notice how the centerman C3 is the backup player to the defenseman in the corner. The role of the centerman is half forward and half defenseman.

The 2-1-2 system is a player specialization system in that each player is a specialist in his duties. In selecting your personnel for the position the following guidelines may be helpful.

W1 and W2 are forwards with the main emphasis on attacking and forechecking. They have free access to roam from side to side of the ice in attacking and forechecking. They must, however, stay in front of the C3, D4 and D5 triangle. Although they can backcheck, it is not their main concern as C3 is the consistent backchecker. With C3 as the consistent backchecker, W1 and W2 can penetrate deep into the offensive end zone and attack aggressively without the concern of positioning for backchecking. W1 and W2 are able to take chances for scoring opportunities.

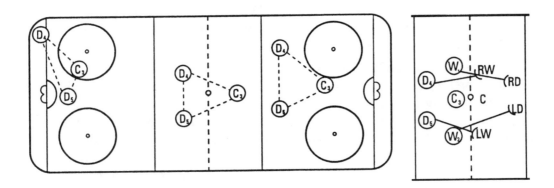

Figure 19-5

Figure 19-6

C3 is half forward and half defenseman with the defensive duties having priority. Defensive duties must have priority for C3 so that there is very little chance of him being caught out of position in the attacking end zone. With W1 and W2 having little backchecking responsibilities C3 must be backup to the attacking W1 and W2 players. C3 is the "quarterback" and will often engineer the attack or the defensive play. He is backup to forwards and defensemen. This player must have good hockey sense, stamina and all round ability for offensive and defensive play. Often it may be of benefit if C3 is a large and strong player. The height may be advantageous to overlooking the entire ice rink. If a centerman under the 3-2 style of play was a strong goal scorer and forechecker it would be best to use this type of centerman as a wing. A defensive style winger from the 3-2 system may be an excellent choice for the centerman position. Very often a defenseman will make a good centerman for the 2-1-2 system. C3 must be disciplined in his positional play and must not wander out of his triangulation with the defensemen.

D4 and D5, the defensemen, must maintain their triangulation with each other and the centerman. They must be disciplined in positional play as they are rarely allowed to penetrate into the offensive end zone. The main duties of the defensemen is to get the puck up to the forwards and centerman and to play defensive hockey.

CHECKING DUTIES

In understanding the 2-1-2 system, it is imperative to realize the checking concept (figure 19-6). This checking system is very simple as each player has the same check throughout the rink. The wings cover the opposing defensemen on their side. This means W1 has the right defenseman and W2 has the left defeseman. The centerman will check the opposing winger and the defensemen will check the opposing wingers on their side.

In the defensive zone (figure 19-7), W1 and W2 are covering their points RD and LD. The defensemen D4 and D5 will be covering their winger checks. C3 naturally covers the opposition's centerman C who is backing up the play.

In forechecking (figure 19-8), the wing W1 will be in the corner with his check RD battling for the puck. As will be noted, all checks are the same in the offensive end zone as they were in the defensive end zone. W2, the far winger, has roaming privileges and may leave his check LD to backup W1 or move to the open space for a passing play. As noted, the wings W1 and W2 are required to use strong coverage of their check in the defensive end zone while in the offensive end zone they are free to roam and leave their check to enhance their attack. Remember, the wings are attackers and goal scorers.

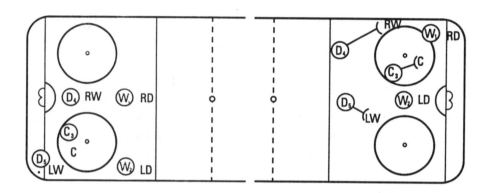

Figure 19-7   Figure 19-8

If the opposition breaks out for a three man rush (figure 19-9), C3, D4 and D5 will have man-on-man coverage with their checks. An advantage of the defensemen and centerman triangle is that if the wingers W1 and W2 are caught deep in the end zone there is still coverage on all the attackers.

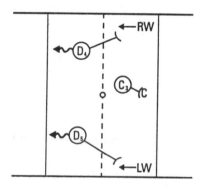

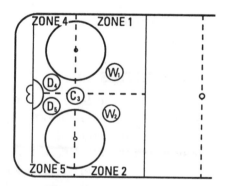

Figure 19-9   Figure 19-10

DEFENSIVE END ZONE PLAY

The defensive end zone (figure 19-10) can be divided into four zones with each player's responsibility as follows:

W1 — zone 1 — pointman in this zone.

W2 — zone 2 — pointman in this zone.

D4 — zone 4 — usually the right winger.

D5 — zone 5 — usually the left winger.

C3 — the backup man to each zone. C3's emphasis is to the defensive end zones 4 and 5. His check will usually be the opposing centerman or the opposing slot man. Although it may look like a zone defense it can be seen that man-to-man coverage is emphasized in the zone.

When the puck is in the corner (figure 19-11), the players will react accordingly:

D4 goes to the puck. If D4 cannot gain puck possession he must prevent his check, usually the right wing in the diagram, from getting by him or getting control of the puck. Often D4 can play the man while C3 goes for the puck. In any event D4 must contain his check to the corner. D4 must not go into the corner with wild abandon and miss the puck and his check.

C3 will back up D4 and will pick up the puck. His check is the backup forechecker who is usually the centerman.

D5, the far defenseman, covers the opposing left winger who is usually in front of the goal net.

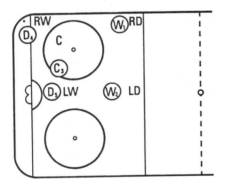

Figure 19-11

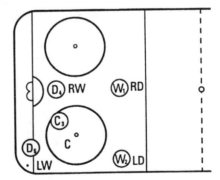

Figure 19-12

As will be noted under the forechecking and backchecking sections D4, D5 and C3 will be covering the same men they picked up in their backchecking responsibilities. There is no confusion as to who covers who when going from forechecking to backchecking to defensive end zone play.

W1 covers the pointman in his zone. He should stay fairly close to the boards so that he can intercept passes up the boards.

W2 will also have the pointman in his zone. Both W1 and W2 must be alert for the quick breakout play.

All players should position themselves between their checks and the goal net. This means that the opposing players have to go through the defender to get to the goal net or slot area. Also, the defender also screens the attacker from the play by positioning himself as such.

When the puck is in the other corner (figure 19-12) the responsibilities are the same. If the puck changes from one corner to the other the defenders simply shift with the puck as there is no change in checking responsibilities.

Most opposing forechecking systems (figure 19-13) will have a man in front of the net RW and a man in the corner on the puck LW. The other forward C is positioned in various positions in between. The in between man C is usually the centerman and he can 1. back up the forechecker in the corner for a two men on the puck style of play; or 2. he can be an extra man in front of the goal net for two men in the slot position; or 3. he can play anywhere in between these two extremes.

Since one defenseman D5 (figure 19-14) is in the corner with the puck and the other defenseman D4 is covering his check in front of the net. C3 is left to make the adjustments on the variable forechecking styles of the opposition. If the opposition has two men on the puck in the corner then C3 moves deeper into the corner to play the backup position and cover the second man C in the corner.

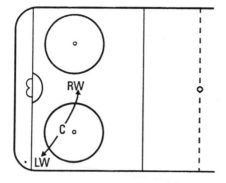

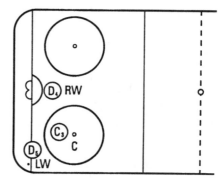

Figure 19-13   Figure 19-14

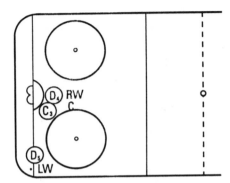

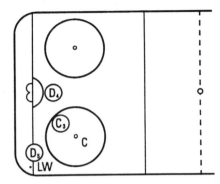

Figure 19-15   Figure 19-16

If the opposition uses one man LW in the corner and two men RW and C in front of the goal net (figure 19-15), then C3 simply makes his adjustment by playing more to the goal net to better cover his man.

If the opposition uses a variation of the two extremes (figure 19-16), C3 can readily adjust to the situation.

If the puck shifts from one corner to the other (figure 19-17), the players move to their comparable positions on the other half of the ice. Notice how there is no shifting of responsibilities or checks as each player maintains his same check.

If the opposing left winger LW carries the puck behind the net (figure 19-18), D5 maintains LW as his check. D4 and C3 should not leave their checks in front of the net unless they can gain positive puck possession. If D4 and C3 leave their checks and are unsuccessful in gaining puck possession then their checks are alone and dangerous in front of the net. LW, the puck carrier, cannot score from behind the goal net so it is imperative to keep his teammates covered in front of the net.

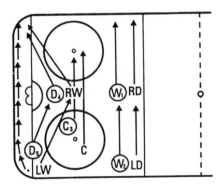

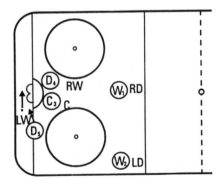

Figure 19-17   Figure 19-18

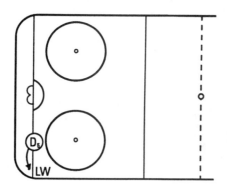
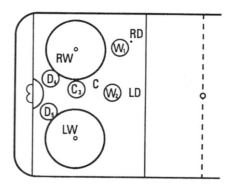

Figure 19-19   *Figure 19-20*

In playing the winger LW in the corner (figure 19-19), the defenseman D5 should contain his check LW in the corner or force him up the boards towards the blue line. D5 must not let his check get by him. D5 must always be between his check and the goal. This strategy is to prevent LW from carrying the puck behind the goal net or towards the goal area and slot. If LW is able to carry the puck behind or towards the goal net, then the opposition is moving towards scoring opportunities.

When the puck is with RD (figure 19-20), W1 will check him and/or force RD into making a play. W1 must not let RD get around him. D4 will check RW, however, he will shade to his goal for defensive purposes. He must not be too close to RW so as to get caught by RW breaking around him to take a pass or rebound. This also applies to the other players in covering their checks.

Average defensive play can often nullify good offensive play, especially in a one-on-one situation (figure 19-21). For player 1 to get around player 2 he must cover more distance than it takes player 2 to cut off his route. As shown above, player 1 requires two units to reach point A or B. Player 2 only requires one unit to reach point A or B and thus check player 1. In defensive play it is important for the defensive player to position himself between his goal and his check. This means his check has to go through him to reach the goal net.

Until puck possession is gained (figure 19-22), the wings W1 and W2 must maintain a close check on the pointmen so that passes to the points cannot be completed. With proper positioning, the wings should be able to prevent passes to the points as one will not pass to a covered man. The teammates of W1 and W2 can dump or pass the puck up to W1 or W2 for the breakout play. In figure 19-22, notice how W1 is in position to cut off the pass to RD and is in position to receive the breakout pass.

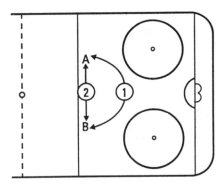

Figure 19-21

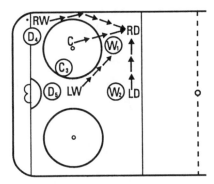

Figure 19-22

BREAKOUT PLAYS

In breaking out of the defensive end zone, the main strategy is to get the puck up to the wings so they can carry the attack quickly out of the end zone. The puck can be advanced to the wings by direct passes or indirect passes along or off the boards. The puck can also be dumped into the neutral ice zone for the wings to pick up. If the puck cannot be advanced to the wings in the defensive end zone, it can be carried up by the defenseman or centerman and advanced to the wings in the neutral ice area of the offensive end zone.

The wings W1 and W2 must be alert to jump into the center ice region to pick up loose pucks or clearing passes (figure 19-23). Notice how W2 cuts to the inside or puck side of his check so as to help block LD from the puck.

W1 can also be involved as the give and go man (figure 19-24). W1 can take the pass from a defenseman or the centerman and give the puck back to his defenseman or centerman or even his winger W2.

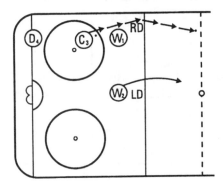

Figure 19-23

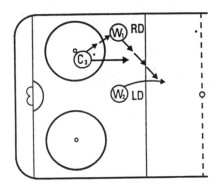

Figure 19-24

Sometimes a clearing pass or bounce pass off the far boards can be an excellent breakout play. The wings W1 and W2 must be alert and move to the puck through the puck side of their checks on the point. (Figure 19-25)

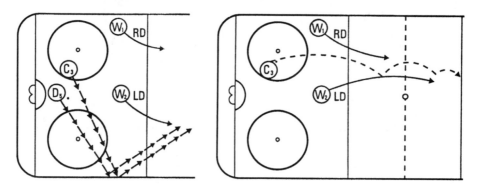

Figure 19-25   Figure 19-26

A quick flip pass between the points (figure 19-26) is an excellent clearing play that can readily turn into an attack. Such a pass requires skill to prevent the puck from sliding too fast for the wingers to pick up or result in an icing call.

Sometimes the defenseman D4 in the corner (figure 19-27) can quickly clear the puck up the boards to W1. W1 should be able to control the puck or redirect the puck to behind his pointman. An alert W2 can pick up the puck for a breakaway or W1 may even to play the puck himself.

If D4 gains control of the puck in the corner (figure 19-28), he can pass the puck to C3 behind the goal net. From this position C3 can pass to a teammate, stop behind the goal net to organize the attack, or rush up the ice. If W2 was to break to the boards he would be in excellent position to receive a pass from C3 for a quick breakout.

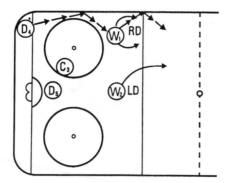

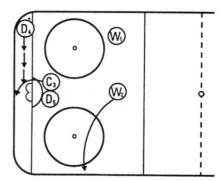

Figure 19-27   Figure 19-28

If D4 has positive puck control in the corner (figure 19-29), D5 can leave his position in front of the goal net and go into his corner to receive a pass from D4. This play can be very effective in breaking out because this moves the puck to open ice area as most of the attackers are on the other side of the ice. D4 can also round the puck off the boards to W2 who breaks towards the boards to pick up the puck.

If the puck is controlled behind the goal net (figure 19-30), C3 or D4 can move to an open corner to receive a pass for a breakout play. On receiving the pass, C3 and D4 can relay the puck up to the wing or skate it out of the end zone. One player should stay in front of the net for defensive purposes or receiving a pass to help in the breakout.

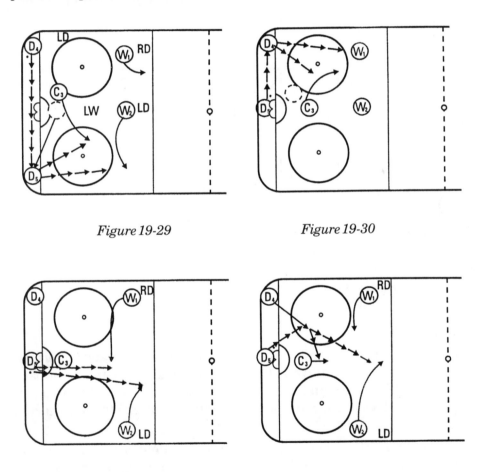

Figure 19-29   Figure 19-30

Figure 19-31   Figure 19-32

A change of pace play when the puck is behind the goal net (figure 19-31) is to have the wingers play wide and high to pull the pointmen to the boards to open up the center ice area. W1 and W2 skate towards each other with W2 angling up ice and W1 continuing straight across so that there is no chance of W1 and W2 colliding. The breakout pass can go to either winger W1 or W2 who is in the most advantageous position.

D5 can also pass to a breaking D4 (figure 19-32) who in turn can relay the pass to C3, W1 or W2.

If the wings are finding difficulty in shaking their checks (figure 19-33), W1 on seeing D4 ready to pass can skate deeper into his end zone to receive a pass from D4. W1 can then relay the pass to C3 skating up the slot.

If one defenseman D4 is behind the goal net with the puck (figure 19-34), C3 and D5 can go into the corners for the breakout pass. With a player in each corner, the breakout plays previously described can be utilized to either side of the ice.

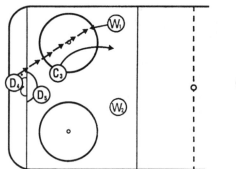

Figure 19-33

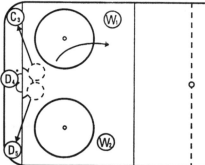

Figure 19-34

THE ATTACK

From the breakout, the team is on the attack. The defensemen and centerman move up the ice and maintain their triangulation. The centerman is the back up man to both wingers and the guaranteed backchecker. The wingers position themselves in the most advantageous situations for goal scoring opportunities.

The positioning of the wings during the attack will depend on the execution of the breakout play. Quite often it will be noted that the wings will be breaking up the ice together on one half of the ice. This is no problem as the wings are not required to be wide on the boards.

Attacking wingers will confront many game situation of one on none, one on one, two on none, two on one, two on two, three on one, three on two, etc. These situations were discussed under Chapter 17: "Basic Team Strategies." The 3 on 2 and full attack are more fully discussed in the section.

THREE ON TWO AND THE FULL ATTACK

The position of the wings for the attack (figure 19-35) will depend on how they breakout of their end zone. In many cases they will be together on one half of the ice and not wide to the boards as in the conventional 3-2 style of play. If the wings separate wide to the boards, the centerman can skate up the middle. When this happens, the conventional attacks of the 3-2 system can be utilized. This section will discuss the strategy when the two wingers are on the same half of the ice. This positioning is most common for the 2-1-2 style of play.

In figure 19-36, W1 and W2 utilize the standard 2-on-1 pass back play. W2 can relay the puck to C3 who is breaking to the goal net or he can shoot on goal. C3 must not get caught deep in the offensive end zone. C3 must make his strike and then retain his triangulation with the defensemen as he is also the guaranteed backchecker.

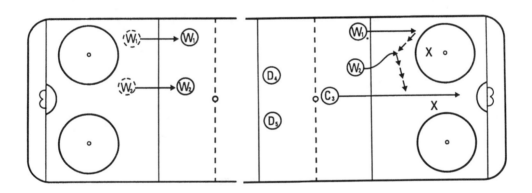

Figure 19-35   *Figure 19-36*

W1, the puck carrier, carries the puck in wide and deep (figure 19-37) and passes to either W2 or C3. W2 or C3 can either shoot on goal or make a passing play with his teammates. It is also possible for W1 to round the puck off the boards to D5 who could drift over and gain puck possession.

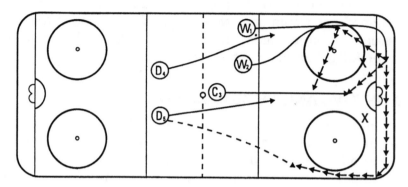

Figure 19-37

When W2, the puck carrier, skates straight at the defender X (figure 19-38), he can make a play to W1 or C3 breaking around or by the defender. W1 and C3 can shoot, make a passing play, play the rebound or set up a screen on the goaltender.

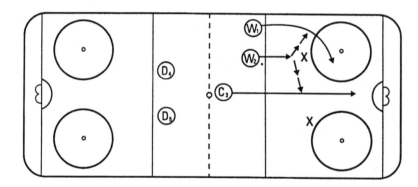

Figure 19-38

The crisscross and pass-back play (figure 19-39) can also be used with C3 as an extra decoy. W2 the puck carrier cuts in front of his defender and pulls the defender X1 with him. W1 cuts behind W2 to receive the pass-back and then he continues to the goal net with the puck. If the other defender X2 moves over to check W1, then W1 can pass back to C3. C3 can go for the net and or a shot on goal.

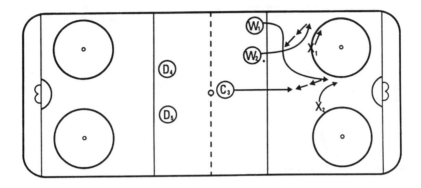

Figure 19-39

If W1 is the puck carrier (figure 19-40), this play will offer variety of play in that the winger on the boards does not try to pull the defender deep into the end zone as in the 2-on-1 situation. Instead W1 cuts to the center ice area and across the defender X to pull him towards the center ice area. As X moves with W1 the puck carrier, W1 passes to W2 breaking towards the boards and around the defender X. W2 continues breaking for the goal net with the puck where he can make a play on goal or a pass to C3 or another teammate.

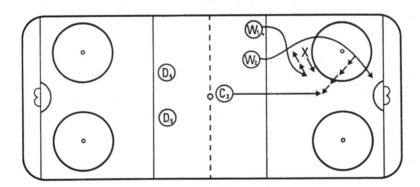

Figure 19-40

If the wings are wide (figure 19-41), C3 can carry the puck over the blue line and setup the double or single crisscross pass-back play. C3 crosses in front of the defenseman X1 and passes back to W1 who can break for the goal net or continue in front of the other defender to give the pass-back play to W2.

With fast breaking wingers (figure 19-42), the simple "dumping in" or "shooting in" can be used. Notice how the angle of the shot can make it easier for W1 or W2 to play the puck.

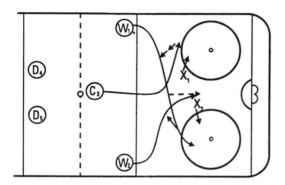

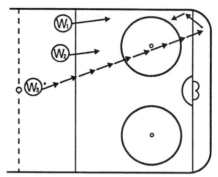

Figure 19-41   Figure 19-42

FORECHECKING

The 2-1-2 formation (figure 19-43) prevails in the forechecking pattern. This formation gives one man on the puck with the backup man not too close to the puck. C3, the backchecker, is the backup man for forechecking in either corner, and for this reason C3 must not penetrate too deep with the risk of being caught or trapped in the offensive end zone. Being trapped in the end zone prevents C3 from his backchecking responsibilities. If W2 goes deep into the corner to help W1, C3 may shift to the slot for scoring opportunities. D4 may penetrate a little deeper to check an opposing winger or centerman from breaking out.

If the puck shifts to the other corner (figure 19-44), a simple shift to the puck side results. Notice how C3 maintains his triangulation with the defensemen D4 and D5. There are many forechecking variations outlined in the Box Strategy Variations section of this chapter that are highly effective with the 2-1-2 system.

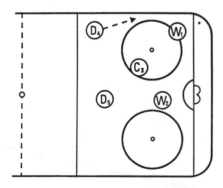

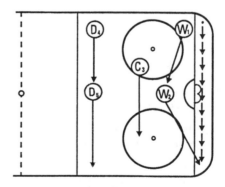

Figure 19-43   Figure 19-44

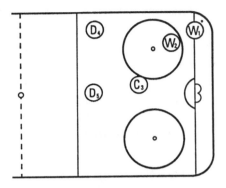

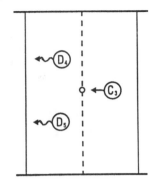

Figure 19-45   Figure 19-46

The conventional styles of forechecking (figure 19-45), as outlined in "Chapter 18:The Three-Two System," will work with the 2-1-2 system. The main difference in using the conventional patterns in the 2-1-2 pattern will be that the two players in the corner will be the wings W1 and W2. This is the result of the wings, when in the defensive end zone, are the first to break out of the end and first to the puck in the offensive end zone.

BACKCHECKING

When the opposition breaks out of their end zone (figure 19-46), D4, D5 and C3 maintain their triangulation as they move to their defensive end. C3 stays in the center lane and backchecks anyone, usually the puck carrier or centerman, in this lane.

The main strategy in backchecking is to force the puck to the side (figure 19-47) if the puck came down the middle. C3 also has coverage of the slot man who is usually the opposition centerman C. This coverage of backchecking gives a one-on-one coverage to each attacker. W1 and W2 must return as quickly as possible to cover their pointmen in the defensive end zone.

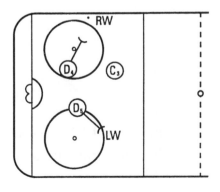

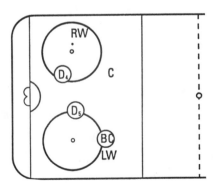

Figure 19-47   Figure 19-48

Under the conventional system with a backchecker taking a wing, the following disadvantages will usually occur on a three man rush. If the backchecker BC covers a wing, then he leaves the centerman C free. D4 has a two-on-one situation which naturally gives the advantage to the two attackers who are very likely to at least get a shot off on goal. D5 is almost out of the play. This situation can be countered very easily and effectively if the backchecker had covered the centerman C instead of covering the winger. By covering the centerman C all defenders have the responsibility to cover only one check.

From the box formation (figure 19-49) with the backchecking emphasis down the slot area an interesting, yet effective system can evolve. This strategy will also work with non-box formations. The idea is to let the defensemen stand up just in front of the blue line to force the opposition into making a play. The defensemen, D4 and D5 force the play at the blue line while the centerman C3 continues to move behind the defensemen to back them up in the event one of them gets beaten. C3 is also in excellent position to chase the puck and be first to the puck if the opposition dumps the puck into the end zone.

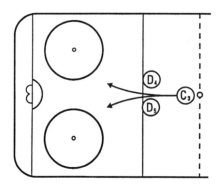

Figure 19-49

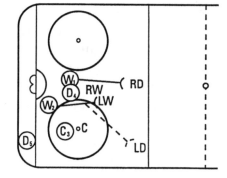

Figure 19-50

FACE-OFFS

Defensive End Zone

The standard face-off formation (figure 19-50) can be used.

With this line up (figure 19-51) everyone checks his normal 2-1-2 checks.

If the opposition does not move LW towards the slot, the setup in figure 19-52 can be used.

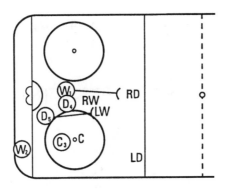

Figure 19-51

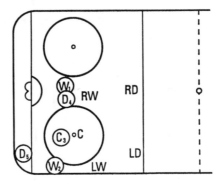

Figure 19-52

Offensive End Zone

Figure 19-53 is the standard setup.

With a good face-off man, the formation in figure 19-54 may have an advantage in getting a man to the net for a screen, rebound or tip-in. W1 and W2 are lined up in front of the net. Notice the space between W1 and W2. D5 moves towards the circle and D4 becomes the backup man.

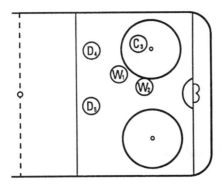

Figure 19-53

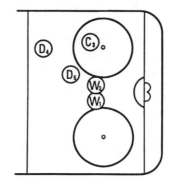

Figure 19-54

If desired, the formation in figure 19-55 may be advantageous in some situations.

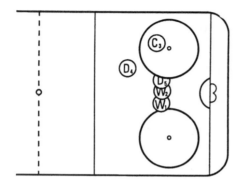

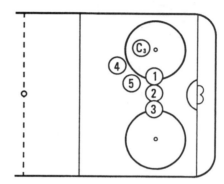

Figure 19-55   *Figure 19-56*

PULLED GOALIE FACE-OFF

If there is a face-off in the opposition's end with only four or five seconds left in the period or game, it is possible to pull the goalie and use an extra attacker on the face-off. The best face-off man, usually C3, takes the draw. 4 and 5 are the best quick shooters. It may be advantageous if the face-off is on the left side to have 4 and 5 with left shots as they will be able to quickly slap a sliding puck without shifting the body for the shot. Players 1, 2 and 3 are the best net scramblers. If they are big and strong it is to the teams advantage (figure 19-56).

PENALTY KILLING - THE 'Y' FORMATION WITH ONE MAN SHORT

Forechecking

The opposition's power play will usually begin behind their goal net (figure 19-57). Note how C3, D4 and D5 maintain their triangle. W1 is the forechecker and he will attempt to forecheck the breakout and try to prevent them from getting organized. As the opposition breaks out, the players pick up their checks as in normal 2-1-2 play. C3 will check the centerman or player breaking down the middle ice lane. C3 will force his check into passing or making a play as most breakout plays have the puck advancing down the center ice lane. D4 and D5 will have the wings as their checks. W1 will usually take the attacking defenseman or wing for backchecking. In most cases, it is best for W1 to check the opposition's attacking defenseman as this will put him into position to cover the strong side of the power play.

Backchecking

As the opposition's power play is breaking down the ice, the player's will position themselves as in figure 19-58. RD is the attacking defenseman and with the wing RW they create the strong side to the power play. W1 checks the strong side. C3 is checking the center ice man, who is usually the puck carrier, and forces the play to the weak side if possible.

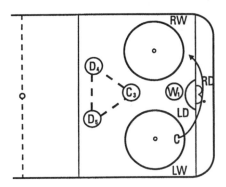 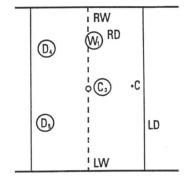

Figure 19-57   Figure 19-58

Defensive End Zone Play

The defensive end zone will set up as in figure 19-59. W1 will adjust to the most dangerous defenseman in relation to puck position. If the puck is in D4's corner, W1 will check the defenseman RD. If the puck is in D5's corner then W1 will have LD as his check. An advantage of this system is that C3 is in the slot to cover the opposing slot man or the most dangerous man in the slot. The three players closest to the goal are covered in a man-to-man or one-on-one situation. D4 and D5 can go into the corners with their checks to fight for puck possession because the slot area is well covered. Under the conventional box style of penalty killing the players do not usually go into the corner to fight for the puck. Fighting for the puck in the corners can often prevent the opposition's power play from getting organized.

When RD has the puck the players position themselves as in figure 19-60. If RD passes to his teammate LD, C3 will drive forward to check LD while W1 rushes to the slotman that C3 was covering. If LD passes back to RD, then the reversed procedure is used with W1 rushing RD and C3 moving back to slot coverage and his check. This rotation between C3 and W1 is similar to the highly effective rotation between a forward and defenseman when playing two men short. This is explained again later. If the rotation is not desired, it is possible to have W1 play both points by moving from one to the other as the situation presents itself.

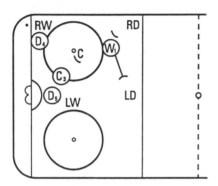
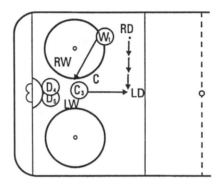

Figure 19-59   *Figure 19-60*

PENALTY KILLING - TWO MEN SHORT

Forechecking and Backchecking

C3, D4 and D5 set up their triangle as in figure 19-61 and backcheck similar to the normal strategy as previously discussed under the one man down system.

Defensive End Zone Play

If the puck is in the corner (figure 19-62), the defenseman D4 moves in for coverage but not deep enough to get caught. The other defenseman covers in front of the goal net while the forward C3 is out to cover the points yet back enough to help cover the opposition's centerman.

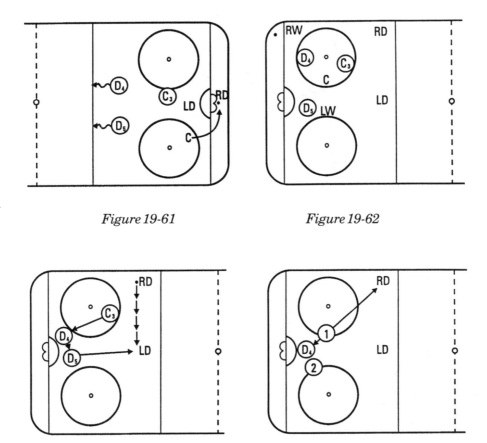

Figure 19-61　　　　　　　　*Figure 19-62*

Figure 19-63　　　　　　　　*Figure 19-64*

If the puck is with RD (figure 19-63), the following setup is used. On the pass to LD from RD, D5 rushes up to check LD and D4 moves over to cover D5's area while C3 rushes back to D4's original position. If LD passes back to RD, then the procedure reverses with C3 moving back out to RD while D4 moves over to give D5 his original position.

A variation of this three man rotation (figure 19-64) is to simply have the middle man remain in the slot while the outside men rush out to the points or retreat to the net depending on puck position. If the right point RD has the puck, 1 moves out for coverage and D4 and 2 cover the slot. If the puck moves to the other point then 2 moves out to cover LD while 1 moves back to the slot position. Players 1 and 2 can be either defensemen or forwards with quick breaking ability and defensive strategy.

If the puck goes to the side and not the points (figure 19-65) then 1 moves out to force the play.

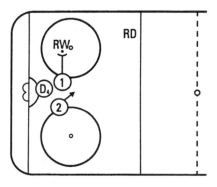

Figure 19-65

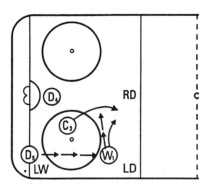

Figure 19-66

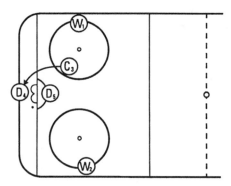

Figure 19-67

PENALTY KILLING BREAKOUT

Hockey teams should not neglect their penalty killing breakout plays. An alert penalty killing team can often breakout and attack against one or two defenders by trapping the opposition's power play attackers deep in the end zone.

Quite often players on the power play become so engrossed with goal scoring attempts that they can very easily be caught deep in the end zone while the penalty killer will break out as in figure 19-66. C3 must be especially quick to break out with W1 for the breakout play.

THE POWER PLAY

The Power Play Breakout

The breakout plays shown under the 2-1-2 system will work for the power play as well, however, the strategy of the centerman going behind the goal net is often used because of its effectiveness. It is similar to the breakout in chapter 16. C3 proceeds behind the goal net to originate the attack (figure 19-67). As C3 begins to round the net, he looks for the opposition's positioning to determine which plan he will take. If C3 has clear access to break out, he will take the puck and if the opposition has his access blocked, he will leave the puck with the defenseman D4.

If C3 takes the puck, he continues around the goal net and up the center ice lane or he can use the give and go with a winger. The give and go is effective to get by a forechecker (figure 19-68).

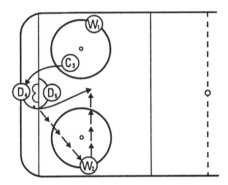 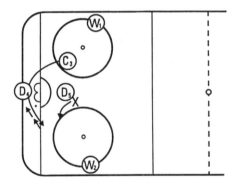

Figure 19-68   *Figure 19-69*

If C3 takes the puck and his access up the ice is blocked (figure 19-69) he simply continues wide to pull the forechecker with him and then passes back to D4 for the breakout.

If C3 leaves the puck for D4, C3 should continue wide into the corner (figure 19-70). The drifting by C3 into the corner may pull the opposition's first forechecker with him and give access to D4 to break out or to pass to W1 and W2. If the forechecker does not follow C3, then C3 will be clear to receive the pass from D4 to initiate the breakout play. On receiving the pass, C3 can carry the puck up the ice or he can pass the puck to W1, W2 or even D5 breaking up the ice.

In setting up after the opposition's icing play (figure 19-71), it is possible to have C3 delay his return to the end zone and then break high and parallel to the blue line. D4 can pass to C3, W1 and/or W2 for the quick breakout play.

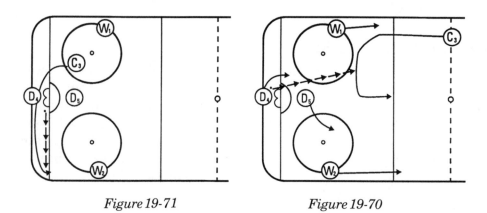

Figure 19-71   *Figure 19-70*

This play is highly effective in trapping a forechecker and leaving him behind the play.

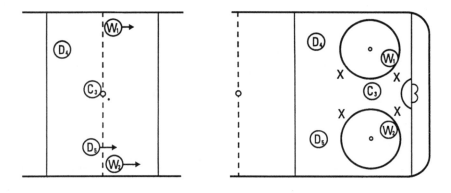

Figure 19-72   *Figure 19-73*

As the breakout progresses towards the offensive end zone (figure 19-72) a strong side pattern can be very effective. The strong side is developed by the defenseman D5 in front of the goal net during the breakout play breaking up the ice inside the winger W2. D5 and W2 can utilize various strategies of the 2-on-1 to beat the opposition's defenders.

The Offensive End Zone Power Play

In figure 19-73, the 2-1-2 pattern will give the standard power play formation. This pattern can be the basis for many variations in the attack.

The formation in figure 19-74 can be called the diamond because of the diamond shaped formation with D4, C3, W1 and D5. Also, C3, D5, W2 and W1 form a diamond. If the puck goes to the other side of the ice the formation is similar. D5 positions himself between the two forward penalty killers. He is in position to move back to defend or move forward to attack the goal. W2 hangs back to cover the open side, or accept passes to open the box and/or attack the goal for passes, rebounds, screens and tip-ins. C3, usually in control of the puck, will initiate the attack. C3 may be considered the quarterback if one prefers that terminology. W1 moves back and forth to set himself clear to receive a pass to set up the attacking play. W1 is also in excellent position for passing to a teammate in the slot. D4, the backup man or safety valve, is also in excellent position to organize a play. A power play unit can and should work the puck to the opposition's weak side or weak defenseman. In selecting the power play personnel, a coach should select the player specific to the duties required or to the personnel of the opposition. It may be advantageous to have D5 as a forward and/or W2 as a defenseman.

Setting up the diamond from the attacking rush (figure 19-75) can be accomplished in several ways. C3 can carry the puck into his position or he can pass it into the end zone while the players are moving into position. In figure 19-75, notice how both defensemen have joined the attack to give two strong sides to the attack.

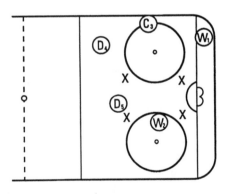
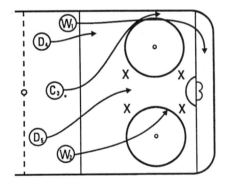

Figure 19-74   *Figure 19-75*

A simple pass to a wing (figure 19-76) can initiate the setting up of the Diamond formation. W1 simply carries the puck along the boards to his position.

In figure 19-77, D5 and W2 should continue to break into the end zone even if the pass is ahead of them. The pass that is ahead of them will deflect into the corner and if D5 and W2 are going full speed they will have a good chance of gaining puck possession in the corner.

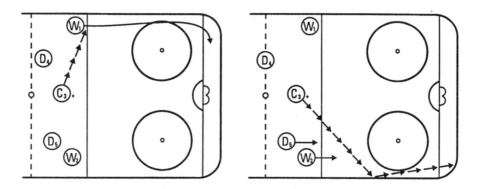

Figure 19-76   *Figure 19-77*

In passing to the strong side (figure 19-78), D5 and W2 can use various 2-on-1 combinations to beat the defender X. Figure 19-78 is an example of a simple 2-on-1 situation. Others combinations are in the following diagrams.

If W2 gets the pass as in figure 19-79, W2 can cut across the defender X to pull X with W2 to open the area for D5 who in turn can receive the pass form W2. If the defender does not move with W2 the puck carrier, then W2 can continue to the goal net.

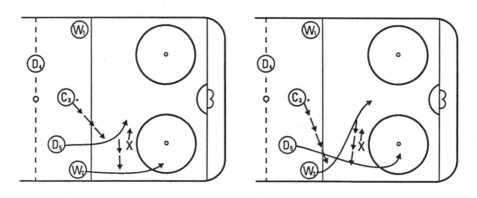

Figure 19-78   *Figure 19-79*

D5 and W2 can use a change of pace (figure 19-80). D5 breaks ahead of W2 and receives the pass from C3. D5 pulls the defender with him and passes back to W2. If the defender X does not move with D5 then D5 may be open to continue to the goal net without passing.

If C3 carries the puck to his position (figure 19-81), W2 and D5 maintain their 2-on-1 pattern as a decoy prior to setting up in their positions. If C3 has difficulty with a penalty killer, C3 can pass back to D4 or C3 could pass to W1 breaking down the boards.

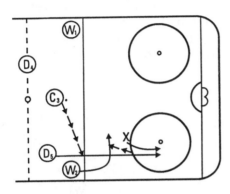

Figure 19-80

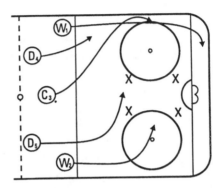

Figure 19-81

Once the diamond is formed (figure 19-82), the following patterns may be used. In selecting W1 and W2 it would be advantageous for them to be of opposite shots to their wing position (e.g. the right wing with a left shot). In the following diagrams it will be noticeable how much easier it is for W1 and W2 to get the quick shot away on goal while taking a pass. C3 passes to D5 breaking to the net. W1 and W2 can play the rebound and/or screen the goalie. W1 is also in position to play the puck to the side or behind the net. An alternative play is C3 passing to W1 who in turn passes to D5 or W2.

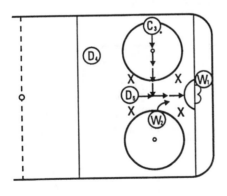

Figure 19-82

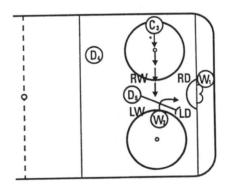

Figure 19-83

In figure 19-83 D5 can move for a pick on the defenseman nearest W2 which is LD. W2 skates behind D5's pick for a pass from C3 or W1 and a play on net.

D5 can also set up the pick on the defensman nearest C3 (figure 19-84) which is RD. C3 can break around the pick using the give and go with W1.

Figure 19-85 is a variation of the previous play. C3 after passing to W1 and breaking through D5's pick on RD, C3 continues to LD. C3 then picks LD so W2 can break around C3 for a pass and play on goal. If C3 does not receive the pass from W1 when he is in the slot then he knows he has to pick the defenseman LD. W2 on seeing C3 does not get the pass then realizes the play is to him so he skates around C3's pick for the pass from W1.

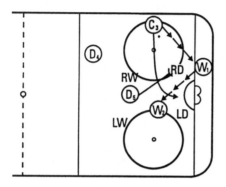
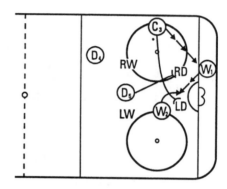

Figure 19-84   Figure 19-85

If penetration of the opposition's penalty killing box becomes too difficult (figure 19-86), the box can be opened up by the above passing pattern. Such passing plays are designed to get the opposition scrambling. C3 passes to D4, who in turn passes to W2 who moves back and wide. W2 can then pass to W1 who has shifted to the other side of the ice. W1 can then make a play with any of his teammates by using the plays previously outlined.

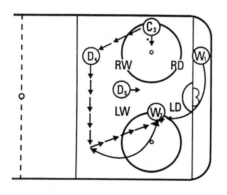
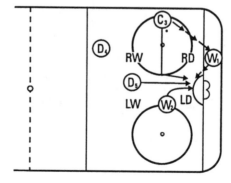

Figure 19-86   Figure 19-87

Figure 19-87 is a good play to flood the slot area. C3 passes to W1 and breaks straight to the slot and cuts sharply to his near goal post. W2 also breaks to the slot and cuts sharply to his near goal post. D5 breaks into the slot between C3 and W2 or an opening in front of the goal net. W1 can pass to either C3, W2, D5 or he can simply dump the puck in front of the goal for a scramble play.

On the play in figure 19-88, W1 passes to C3 and skates behind the goal net. Once W1 is behind the net, W2 breaks to the far goal post in front of the goalie to screen the goalie and to pull the defenseman LD with him. W1 breaks around the goal net and quickly slaps the pass from C3 to the goal net. The goalie is very vulnerable on this play as he is positioned for C3, the puck carrier, and the back of his goal is open.

A variation of the diamond formation (figure 19-89) is to use the 3-on-2 rush from the side. D4, C3 and W1 simply employ 3-on-2 strategy against RW and RD.

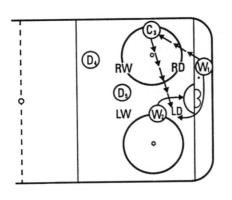

Figure 19-88

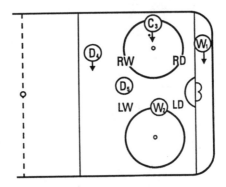

Figure 19-89

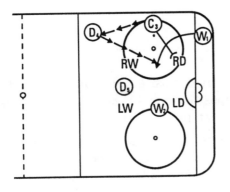

Figure 19-90

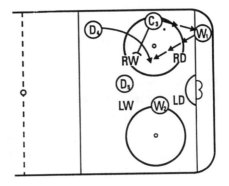

Figure 19-91

The use of pick plays is illustrated in figure 19-90. C3 passes to D4 and picks the defenseman RD. W1 cuts around the pick and receives the pass from D4.

The same pick pattern as previously illustrated will also work to the other side (figure 19-91). C3 passes to W1 who in turn passes to D4 breaking around C3's pick on RW. On this 3-on-2 pick play, the rule is to set the pick on the player farthest from the pass receiver. C3 passes to his left and picks to his right. The non-pass-receiver is free to cut around the pick for the pass. The 3-on-2 pick play (figure 19-92) is highly effective from the blue line. C3 passes to D5 and then picks the farthest defender RW so that D4 can cut around the pick and receive the pass from D5. W1 and W2 should move to the net for playing the puck and to keep the defensemen busy. This play can run with the initial pass to D4. The initial pass will determine who will take the shot on goal. For example, if D4 has a better shot than D5, then the initial pass should be to D5.

Another power play formation is the cross formation in figure 19-93. This strategy will give variety to the power play attack. W1, W2 and D5 play the area outside the box while D4 and C3 are the slotmen. D4 and C3 are in excellent position for screens, tip-ins and rebounds. In most cases, it is more advantageous if C3 and D4 are big and strong for the goal mouth scrambles.

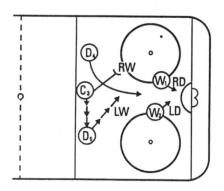
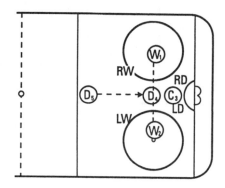

Figure 19-92   Figure 19-93

When puck control is lost (figure 19-94), the opposite or far winger shifts to become a defenseman in the event the opposition does breakout. D4 becomes a backchecker and forms the backchecking triangle with D5 and W2.

Numerous passing combinations can be utilized and it would be too repetitive to diagram them all. C3 and D4 can cause great havoc and confusion by playing tandem in the slot. Sometimes W1 and W2 can also move into the slot. The players must be alert and not so goal hungry that they get caught deep in the end zone and are unprepared for the opposition's breakout play.

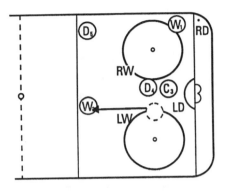 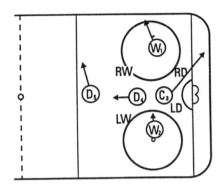

Figure 19-94   *Figure 19-95*

The cross formation lends itself to more shooting on goal and playing rebounds and scrambles because of the overload in the slot area. The diamond formation has players breaking into the slot through various passing plays. The cross formation may be considered more of a static formation while the diamond is more of a mobile attack. A coach must evaluate his personnel to determine which formation may best suit his personnel. It would be best, however, to incorporate both strategies to add more confusion to the enemy.

Shifting from the cross to the diamond (figure 19-95) can easily be executed during actual play. W1 has the puck and signals for the change in strategy. D5 moves to the boards on the puck side. C3 shifts to behind the goal line to the puck side. D4 moves between the two forwards LW and RW. W2 moves a little closer to the puck. To shift from the diamond to the cross, the procedure is just reversed.

THE FIRST MAN ON THE PUCK AND THE SECOND MAN ON BACKUP RULE

If a team has versatility in its forwards, the coach may prefer to use the first man on the puck and the second man backup rule. The strategy and playing of the 2-1-2 system remains the same except that there is an interchange of roles among the forwards when following this rule.

Defensive End Zone Play

Figure 19-96 is based on the rule of "first man on the puck and the second man backup". The first backchecker W2 takes the role of the centerman, while the second backchecker C3 will back up the play by covering the pointman. The third man back is W1 and is high in the slot and covering the point man. When the puck is in the corner, W2 now has the role of the centerman as he backs up D5 in the corner. You will notice how the players are in the same position as just the names are different.

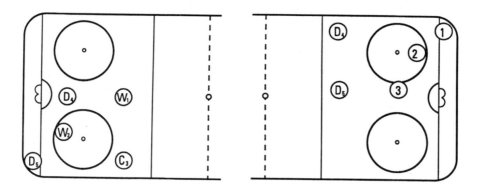

Figure 19-96   *Figure 19-97*

Forechecking

In forechecking (figure 19-97), the same rule applies. The first player 1 is on the puck, the second forechecker 2 is the backup man and the third forechecker 3 is high in the slot and takes the role of the centerman by triangulating with D4 and D5.

The 2-1-2 system can also use a non-roving winger strategy (figure 19-98). This means that the wingers stay on their own half of the ice. With this rule the centerman C3 becomes the first man in or the back up man to each side of the ice.

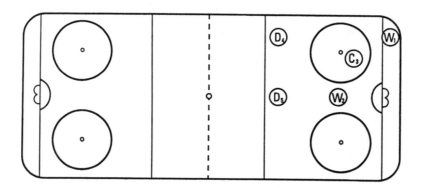

Figure 19-98

20

BOX STRATEGY VARIATIONS

There are many variations to the basic 2-1-2 system. The variation used will depend on the personnel on the team. In analyzing the variations, one must not use the set of rules that govern conventional play like the 3-2 system. These systems are different but effective. Pieces, patterns and strategies in this chapter may be adapted to the 2-1-2 system, or any other system, very easily.

1-2-2 SYSTEM

Defensive End Zone

The 1-2-2 system (figure 20-1) derives its name from the above positioning. The corner of the box nearest the puck moves out to the puck while a rotation fills the corners vacated. With the puck in the corner, D5 moves out to play the puck. W2 slides down to take D5's place and C3 moves into W2's place. The box part of the 1-2-2 formation plays much like the penalty killing box strategy only a little more aggressively to the puck.

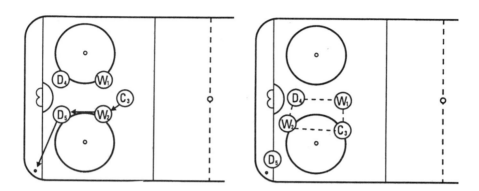

Figure 20-1   *Figure 20-2*

With the puck in the corner (figure 20-2), the players will be in this formation.

If LW passes the puck to LD (figure 20-3), the rotation is as diagramed. D5 returns to his defensive corner while W2 replaces C3 who is rushing LD.

If the pointman LD has puck possession (figure 20-4), C3 covers the point LD. If LD makes a pass to RD, then W1 moves out on RD, W2 takes W1's place and C3 takes W2's place.

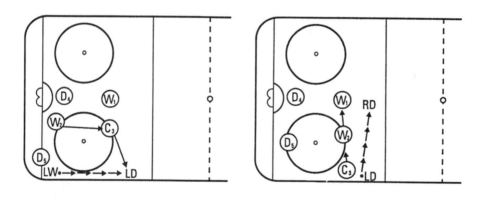

Figure 20-3   *Figure 20-4*

1-2-2 Breakout Plays

The 1-2-2 pattern lends itself for a quick one man breakout (figure 20-5). This formation could be used when a team is trying to get a man behind the points for a quick breakaway pass. C3's objective is to sneak behind the points for the pass or C3 and a wing W1 or W2 could team up so that one of is able to sneak behind the points.

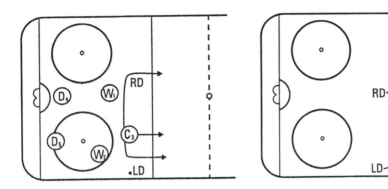

Figure 20-5   Figure 20-6

C3's positioning (figure 20-6) and trying to sneak behind the points can often pull a pointman over the blue line and out of the end zone. Even if C3 does not receive a pass, his positioning for pulling the point man out of the end zone can be very effective in helping to kill the opposition's attack. Once a pointman is pulled out of the end zone, the end zone becomes a 4-on-4 situation. C3 in position A (figure 20-6) is wide open for a pass. C3 in position B is a problem to the pointmen LD and RD.

1-2-2 Forechecking

The wing W1 and defenseman D4 on the side of the puck do the forechecking (figure 20-7) while the centerman C3 consistently remains in the slot no matter what side the puck is in or moved to. With the puck in the corner, the near winger W1 moves in and on the puck. D4, the near defenseman, plays the winger LW on the boards. D5 hangs back as the safety valve.

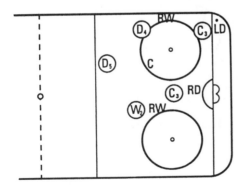

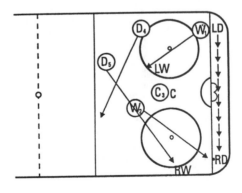

Figure 20-7   Figure 20-8

If the puck moves to the other side (figure 20-8), the near winger W2 moves in on RD, and D5, the near defenseman, plays the opposition's near winger RW. The far defenseman D4 becomes the safety valve while W1 backs off the corner to cover LW.

1-2-2 and 1-4 Forechecking

A forechecking variation (figure 20-9) is to send one man in deep with the two wingers back with the defense to assure two backcheckers. This is referred to as a 1-2-2 or a 1-4 forechecking system depending on the positioning of the wingers W1 and W2. If the wingers are positioned as in figure 20-9, it is still a 1-2-2 system with the forwards playing wide. If the wingers move to positions A and B, then it is called a 1-4 system. C3 is the only forechecker, and he backchecks the centerman or the player in the center ice lane. The other players wait for the opposition to breakout and then they will pick up their checks.

Most of the breakout plays and defensive end zone play in the 2-1-2 box strategy are utilized in the 1-2-2 system. The attack and forechecking principals are almost the same.

2-3 BOX AND 3-2 BOX

Defensive End Zone

Two minor variations (figure 20-10) of a box strategy are the 2-3 box and the 3-2 box. The strategy is much the same as the 2-1-2 with an emphasis on the positioning of C3. In the 3-2 box, C3 is positioned high in his defensive slot. In the 2-3 box, C3 is positioned low in the slot. The choice of where to play C3 will depend on the personnel on the team and the opposition's style of play.

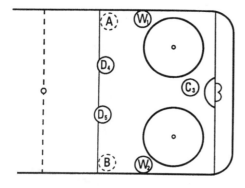

Figure 20-9

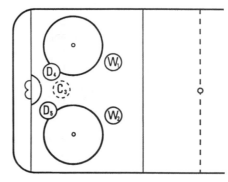

Figure 20-10

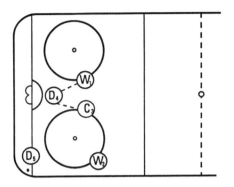

Figure 20-11

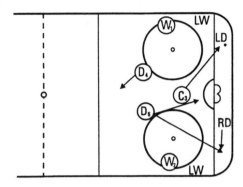

Figure 20-12

The 3-2 box Defensive End Zone

With the puck in the corner (figure 20-11), the defenseman D5 plays the puck. D4, W1, and C3 play an inverted triangle. This formation gives very strong slot coverage, but it leaves only one man in the corner.

3-2 Forechecking

With the 3-2 forechecking system, the wings W1 and W2 cover the opposition's wings. Both defensemen move deep into the end zone and form a triangle with C3. The centerman attacks the puck carrier LD while the far defenseman D5 moves in on the opposition's other defenseman RD, who may be in front of the net or behind the goal crease line for a pass. The defenseman D4 backs off the play to become the safety valve (figure 20-12).

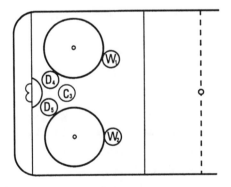

Figure 20-13

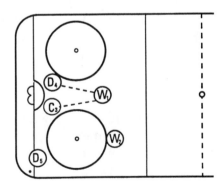

Figure 20-14

2-3 Box in the Defensive End Zone

In the 2-3 box (figure 20-13), C3 is positioned low in the slot.

When the puck is in the corner (figure 20-14), D5 plays the puck while C3, D4, and W1 have slot coverage. W2 is playing his pointman.

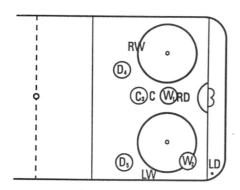

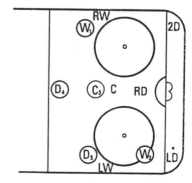

Figure 20-15   Figure 20-16

2-3 Box Forechecking

The 2-3 forechecking system is a pressing style of play (figure 20-15). The near winger W2 plays the puck carrier LD in the corner and tries to force the play. The other winger W1 picks up his check, RD the other defenseman, in front of the goal or behind the goal crease. The centerman C3 plays the man in the center ice area which will usually be the opposition's centerman C. The wings are covered by the defensemen D4 and D5. The near defenseman D5 moves into the opposition's near winger LW. D4 is the safety valve on the play but covers his wing RW on the boards if the puck goes to the other side of the ice.

If the puck moves to the other side of the ice (figure 20-16), D4 moves in on RW while D5 backs off to become the safety valve.

1-3-1 Forechecking

This is a pressing system with the wingers and defensemen alternating responsibilities. The near winger W2 plays the puck carrier (figure 20-17). The centerman C3 plays the center ice area and the opposition's centerman C. The near defenseman D5 moves in to play the opposition's near winger LW. D4 is the backup man or safety valve. The far winger W1 covers the opposition's winger RW. The opposition's far defenseman RD is left open.

If LD passes to RD (figure 20-18), W1 moves in to check RD. D4 shifts to cover RW while D5 moves back as a safety valve. W2 moves up to cover LW.

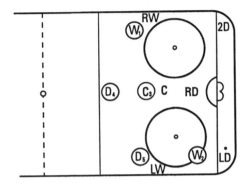

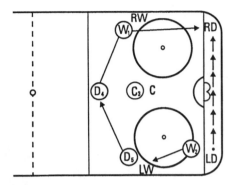

Figure 20-17   *Figure 20-18*

2-2-1 SYSTEM

The 2-2-1 system (figure 20-19) can be a very effective style of play. To outline its positional play in detail would be repetitious from the previous strategies discussed. This system is similar to the 2-1-2 system except that C3 is moved back as the last defensive post or safety valve. D4 and D5 are moved slightly ahead so that their new role is half forward and half defensemen. C3 is strictly defensive. Depending on the coach's philosophy and personnel, the wingers can have roaming privileges or they can remain to their side of the ice and work with their near defenseman.

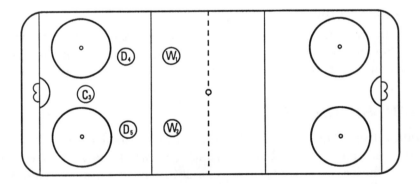

Figure 20-19

21

ROTATIONAL STRATEGIES

Rotational strategies can be used with the 3-2 system or the box systems. The rotational strategies can be effective if the personnel are skilled in a variety of positions. The four main rotational strategies are:

1. Only the forwards rotate.

2. The wings and defensemen on the same side rotate.

3. The center and defensemen rotate.

4. All five players rotate.

Rotational strategies are utilized mostly in the end zones although crossing patterns in the mid-ice area can be developed. Rotational strategies are probably most effective during the attack or the forechecking patterns.

FORWARDS ROTATION

Rotation patterns (switching of roles) has been described in previous sections and chapters. A basic forward rotation pattern is when the puck moves to the other side of the ice. W1 shifts to the other side to back up W2 as W1 has quicker access than C3 to the other corner. W1 has become the centerman and the centerman C3 becomes the winger.

In the event W2 plays the puck behind the goal net (figure 21-2), W2 and the backup man C3 switch positions with C3 moving right over to cover the opposition's wing LW while W2 becomes the new centerman.

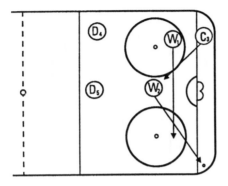

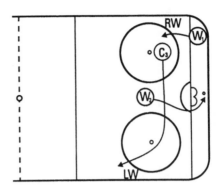

Figure 21-1   *Figure 21-2*

Often when a winger W1 is breaking for the net ahead of his teammates (figure 21-3), it is advantageous for W1 to continue into the opposite corner to be first on the puck. This often happens after the winger's shot on goal is deflected into the far corner. When this happens, C3 shifts over to take W1's wing position, and W2 becomes the new centerman.

With a winger W1 breaking deep to the goal net or into the opposite corner (figure 21-4), the rotational pattern works quickly into backchecking duties. There is no stopping and starting of the players when returning to backchecking duties. Quick turns by C3 and W2 will put them into their new backchecking lanes. C3 takes W1's lane, W2 becomes the new centerman, and W1 has W2's lane. Notice the direction of the turn by C3 and W2 is opposite to the direction of W1's turn.

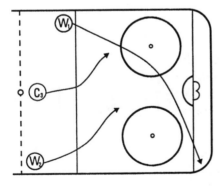

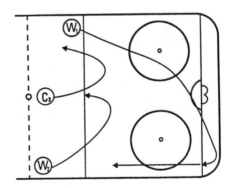

Figure 21-3   *Figure 21-4*

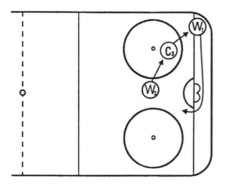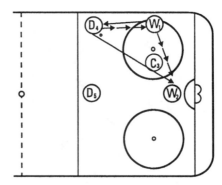

Figure 21-5   *Figure 21-6*

Often the corner man W1 can break to behind the goal net and come out the other side of the goal net. On this pattern, W1 becomes the new W2. W2 now becomes C3, and C3 becomes the new W1 winger. This is a complete circle rotation and can be effective and confusing to the opposition. It is possible for this rotation to rotate several times. This pattern can also be effective in a forechecking pattern (figure 21-5).

WING AND DEFENSEMAN ROTATE

This rotation pattern (figure 21-6) is excellent when defensemen break for the goal net or other scoring opportunities. If the defenseman D4 is breaking for the net, the wing W1 must cover for him by taking D4's position on defense. An effective give and go pass pattern is for D4 to pass to W1 and then break to the goal net for a return pass from W1. W1, after passing, takes D4's original position on defense. D4 becomes W1 after the play is completed.

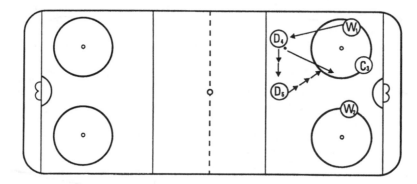

Figure 21-7

The same rotation (figure 21-7) also takes place if D4 uses the give and go with the other defenseman. D4 passes to D5 and breaks for the net to take the return pass. W1 rotates to D4's original position.

Similar rotation (figure 21-8) can apply to the far winger and far defenseman. D5 breaks for the goal and W2 covers D5's original position.

CENTER AND DEFENSEMEN ROTATE

This type of rotation (figure 21-9) is similar to the wing and defense rotation except that it is the centerman C3 rotating with the defenseman. In this type of rotation, it is the centerman's responsibility to cover for his defensemen when the defenseman breaks for the goal or penetrates for forechecking duties.

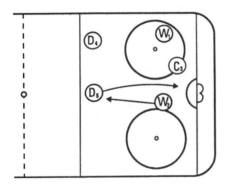

Figure 21-8

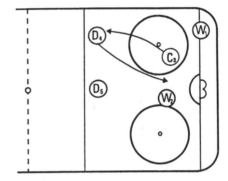

Figure 21-9

ALL PLAYERS ROTATE

Figure 21-10 shows a three man rotational pattern. When D4 breaks into the end zone, W1 takes his position and C3 moves to W1's old position. The players simply rotate in a circular pattern.

The rotation pattern in figure 21-11 occurs in the slot area. The defenseman D5 breaks to the far goal post for a play on the net. The centerman C3 covers for D5 and W2 becomes the new centerman. After his rush, D5 becomes the winger.

In forechecking (figure 21-12), the rotation pattern can be used for quick effective coverage. If the puck moves to the other corner, the near wing W2 moves in to play the man or the puck. His defenseman D5 also moves in to become the backup man. The far defenseman D4 continues across the ice to become the near defenseman. The backup forechecker C3 moves to become the other defenseman, while W1 moves into the slot position.

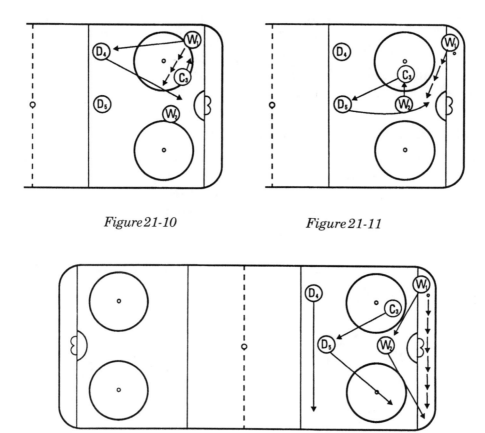

Figure 21-10   Figure 21-11

Figure 21-12

If the defenseman D4 is well up with the play (figure 21-13), it may be advantageous to have D4 continue in deep while the centerman C3 takes D4's position on defense.

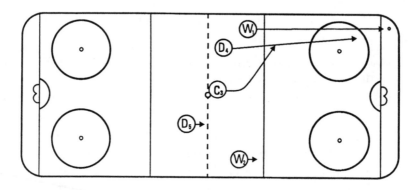

Figure 21-13

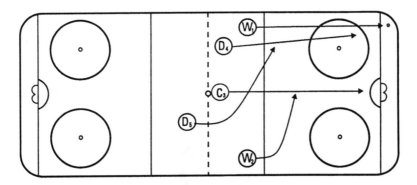

Figure 21-14

With the puck in the corner (figure 21-14) and with W1 and D4 breaking for the puck area, C3 can break for the goal to have a slot man if puck possession is gained. D5 and W2 shift over to become defensemen.

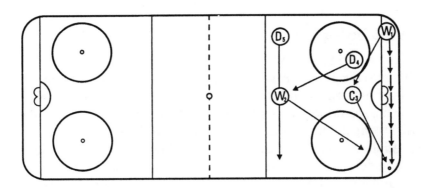

Figure 21-15

Figure 21-15 is the rotation for when the puck moves to the other corner. The centerman C3 goes to the corner while his defenseman W2 backs him in the corner. D5 moves to the far boards to become the near defenseman, and D4 rotates back to his defense position.

22

WINGER ON WINGER

With a Sinking or Tandem Defense

The winger on winger strategy involves a man-on-man coverage by the wings with mostly zone coverage by the other players. The effectiveness of this strategy is enhanced by the sinking defenseman or tandem defense. The criteria for the selection of this strategy would be excellent style of play for a team with strong defensemen and centermen. If the wings are weak offensively, especially at putting the puck in the net, then it may be best to have them play a strong defensive role. If the opposition has good wingers, then this strategy may counter the wingers strengths as the opposition wings will have constant coverage. The wings must be very disciplined in their defensive role and coverage of their checks. If the wings roam, get goal hungry, or inattentive, the strategy will break down. The play of the wings is the key to this system.

Defensive End Zone

When the puck is in the corner (figure 22-1), the near defenseman D5 moves to the corner. The two wingers W1 and W2 cover their wings. The far wing W1 is in the slot and will cover his check RW as well as the far point RD, as D4 can take coverage of RW. W2 is the near winger and covers his check LW. The centerman C3 has the near point LD.

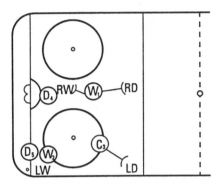

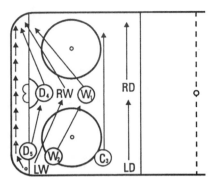

Figure 22-1   Figure 22-2

If the puck shifts to the other corner (figure 22-2), the wingers W1 and W2 still maintain their checks. D4 moves into the corner to play the puck against RW who will also break for the corner. The centerman C3 shifts to the far side to cover the near defenseman RD. W2, the far winger, is now in the slot and must cover his check LW who is also in the slot and LD the far defenseman. D5 is now in front of the net and can take coverage of LW to help W2. The defensive play and end zone coverage is much like the basic 3-2 strategy, and the rotation is much the same. The breakout plays for the winger-on-winger system are much the same as other breakout plays discussed in previous chapters.

Offensive End Zone Play

The centerman C3 does the initial forechecking (figure 22-3) as the wingers cover their wings. Notice the positioning of W1 and W2 as it is very essential to the system. W1 and W2 always play their checks so that they have to look through their checks to see the puck. By doing this, they block their check access to the goal. W1 and W2 always maintain themselves so that they are between their check and their goal. If RW or LW were to get the puck, they would have to go through W1 or W2 to advance to the goal. This positioning of W1 and W2 makes it easier to bodycheck their checks and to stay between their goal and their checks.

A team that relies on their wings for the breakout may have trouble against the winger-on-winger system. W1 and W2's main responsibility is defensive. They can leave their checks to score but such offensive play must be restricted to very certain scoring opportunities. If W1 and W2 become too offensive then the strategy is ineffective. W1 and W2 must not get caught out of position. The scoring opportunities are mostly in the hands of the centerman and the sinking defenseman.

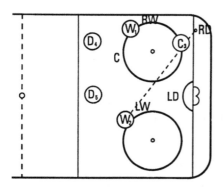

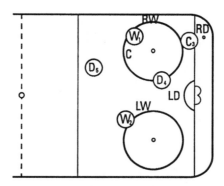

Figure 22-3   Figure 22-4

The use of the sinking defenseman or tandem defense (figure 22-4) will give strength to the attack as well as an extra backup man for forechecking. The sinking defenseman is the defenseman that sinks deep into the slot area. The sinking defenseman can be the same player all the time, the near defenseman or the far defenseman. The coach can make this decision. In diagram 21-4, D4 is the near defenseman and he is the sinking defenseman. D5, the far defenseman, is the safety valve. Everyone has a man to cover and with both wingers covered, it is not dangerous to sink the defenseman. The opposition's centerman C can be covered by the safety valve D5.

The sinking defenseman D4 has several alternatives (figure 22-5). D4 can back up C3. D4 can cut off the access of a player or the puck from going behind the goal net. D4 can check LD. D4 is in good position to forecheck, screen, rebound, tip-in and shoot on goal.

If the puck is moved quickly to the other corner (figure 22-6), D4 can go with LD into the corner. D4 should go into the corner and play LD as this will keep all players with their same checks. If D4 is unable to play LD, then it may be wise for D4 to retreat and pick up LD later.

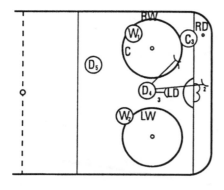

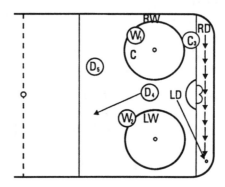

Figure 22-5   Figure 22-6

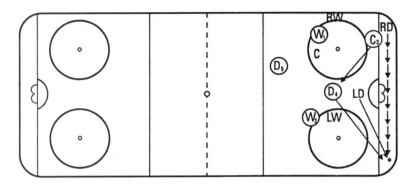

Figure 22-7

Another approach to the change of corners (figure 22-7) is to switch D4 and C3. If the puck switches to the other corner, D4 can move in to the puck while C3 takes the slot position and becomes the sinking defenseman. D4 is now the centerman. If the opposition breaks out, C3 and D4 must remain in their new roles and backcheck as such.

Backchecking

If the opposition does break out (figure 22-8), the players assume normal backchecking duties. In backchecking, D4 can stay in the middle to form a tandem defense with D5. The tandem defense gives strong coverage to the slot and middle ice area, the most dangerous areas of the rink. With a tandem defense, the puck carrier may get by one defenseman but the next defenseman is there to take him. When the defense plays parallel to the blue line then the puck carrier beats both defensemen if he gets around one of the defensemen.

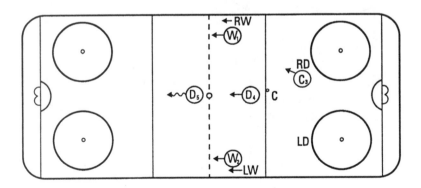

Figure 22-8

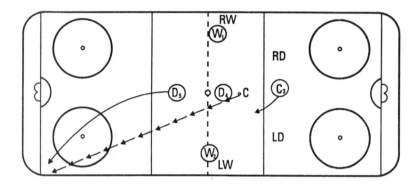

Figure 22-9

With the wings covered (figure 22-9), the defense can be more aggressive and force the play. If the opposition's center C has the puck, then D4 can rush or attack C to force the play. If C shoots the puck into the end zone, then D5 should be first on the puck. C3 plays the most dangerous player. Again, it is imperative that the wings do their checking very proficiently.

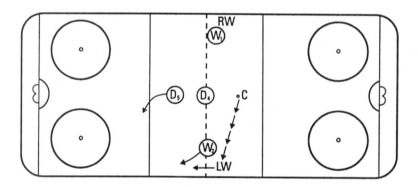

Figure 22-10

If the opposition's centerman C passes to his wing LW (figure 22-10), W2 can check LW by playing the body and D5 can move over to pick up the puck. D4 continues backwards as a defenseman by taking D5's place.

MASTERS PRESS

DEAR VALUED CUSTOMER,

Masters Press is dedicated to bringing you timely and authoritative books for your personal and professional library. As a leading publisher of sports and fitness books, our goal is to provide you with easily accessible information on topics that interest you written by the most qualified authors. You can assist us in this endeavor by checking the box next to your particular areas of interest.

We appreciate your comments and will use the information to provide you with an expanded and more comprehensive selection of titles.

Thank you very much for taking the time to provide us with this helpful information.

Cordially,
Masters Press

Areas of interest in which you'd like to see Masters Press publish books:

☐ COACHING BOOKS
   Which sports? What level of competition?

☐ INSTRUCTIONAL/DRILL BOOKS
   Which sports? What level of competition?

☐ FITNESS/EXERCISE BOOKS
   ☐ Strength—Weight Training
   ☐ Body Building
   ☐ Other

☐ REFERENCE BOOKS
   what kinds?

☐ BOOKS ON OTHER
   Games, Hobbies
   or Activities

Are you more likely to read a book or watch a video-tape to get the sports information you are looking for?

I'm interested in the following sports as a participant:

I'm interested in the following sports as an observer:

Please feel free to offer any comments or suggestions to help us shape our publishing plan for the future.

Name _____ Age _____

Address _____

City _____ State _____ Zip _____

Daytime phone number _____

BUSINESS REPLY MAIL

FIRST CLASS MAIL   PERMIT NO. 1317   INDIANAPOLIS IN

POSTAGE WILL BE PAID BY ADDRESSEE

MASTERS PRESS

2647 WATERFRONT PKY EAST DR

INDIANAPOLIS IN 46209-1418

NO POSTAGE
NECESSARY
IF MAILED
IN THE
UNITED STATES